F.I.R.E. /
The Merchant

Life Experiences & Advice

By
Gaylen K. Bunker

Contents

Acknowledgements

I want to express appreciation for the generous contributions made by my wife, Diane, who has read and reread the manuscript many times and given extremely valuable input. Thanks must be extended to my daughter-in-law, Casey Bunker, for all her work to improve this manuscript.

I also want to thank the many others who read the manuscript and offered comments that were very valuable.

Thank You
Gaylen K. Bunker

Introduction

During my teaching years, I have drawn upon my personal work experience to illustrate finance and accounting principles in the classroom. I tried to bring to life textbook concepts and provide students with a better understanding of financial controls and how they are applied. It appeared that students enjoyed having a glimpse into the world of work as I experienced it.

The journey of recording these incidents began as I focused on the most important control elements for any business. I used the acronym FIRE to help students quickly recall them: fixed assets, inventories, receivables, and excess earnings.

After writing each story, the work appeared to be too sterile for the average reader. However, I continued to flesh out the fabric of my experiences around these major building blocks. As Warren Buffett said, "It is easier to entertain than to educate."

I soon realized that, in many respects, the stories focused on the negative aspects of business. The truth is that my forty years of work experience has been a complete joy. I have loved the people I worked with and the responsibilities I've had. I'm sorry if the joy, success, and love for those individuals is not more apparent.

Gaylen K. Bunker

The Marble Street Bakery

I really wondered if I could measure up and be worth anything when it came to working for pay. One of my first opportunities came while I was still in high school. I landed a job at the Marble Street Bakery a few blocks from my house. I was responsible for cleaning the pots, pans, trays, and baking equipment. After school, I put an apron on and began washing in two large sinks.

After a few days one of the old bakers was waiting for me when I arrived. He said he wanted to see me work, so I went through my normal routine. Not long after I started he stopped me and said, "You'll never get anywhere that way. You're holding back too much. You have to dive right in and get wet."

I took the message to heart. I went home after school, changed into work clothes, left for the bakery, put on the apron, and let the water fly. I even tried to do extra work to impress the bakers so they could see I wasn't a slacker. When finished washing, I would sweep the floor and wash the windows. Since I was paid by the hour, I felt I was really earning my pay.

I must have been successful because they asked me to work full-time that summer assisting the bakers. I took to it like a duck to water, except for one thing: I had to be at work at 4:00 a.m. That was the most painful thing in the world for a teenager; to sacrifice summer evenings to be up that early in the morning.

In some ways I really grew to love that job. I was good at measuring the dough for each loaf, molding it into balls, tossing it into the roller, placing it in the pans, and getting it in and out of the oven. They used to call me "hot hands" because I moved the bread so quickly.

I was not the innovator I would later become. A lot of things were taken for granted, such as the fixed assets (ovens, mixing machines, etc.) that were required to support the operation and the inventory of raw materials (flour, yeast, oil, etc.) and finished goods (the bread). They were there and didn't seem to need any control.

Key Point

- This is growth: first resist; then submit; and finally, embrace.

Uptown Department Store

In 1967, early in my freshman year of college, I obtained a job at the Uptown Department Store as a stock boy. I would go to school in the morning and work in the afternoon. One day my boss told me to go to the men's furnishings stock room and organize the inventory. When I arrived in the basement there were packages of shirts, pajamas, socks, ties, and underwear everywhere. I spent the next couple of days organizing the merchandise. You could walk in and find anything you needed. I guess this was when I first thought about an organized and controlled inventory.

Afterward, Lew, the head of the men's furnishings department, asked me if I wanted to work on the floor as a sales associate. I said "sure," put away my smock, put on a dress shirt and tie, and began selling. It was great fun, particularly at Christmas when everything went nuts. It was very busy and I loved it. Truck after truck of new merchandise came in and shoppers were everywhere. It was crazy to see the door-crashers who would literally burst through the doors in the morning and run down the aisles. Almost all of them were women.

When Christmas and the January White Sale passed, we would go to the stock room and package the unsold merchandise and ship it back to the vendor. We did this prior to taking an inventory count. I wondered if some merchandise floated around in transit somewhere, never counted by the vendor who wanted to record it as being sold, nor counted by the retailer who didn't want it on the books as a cost. On inventory days, we would close the store, tag all the shelves, and count merchandise.

Managing inventory on an ongoing basis was a strange thing. We had a whole bin of socks that were never sold at full price and only brought out from the store room when a sale was advertised. They were referred to as "sale socks."

It seemed to me that being the buyer for the department was a big responsibility. They had to go to the New York markets and purchase what they judged the public would actually want to buy. If they guessed wrong, there would be a buildup of excess merchandise that wouldn't move. It was probably easier than I imagined. I'm sure the trends in New York were universally agreed on by the general society of buyers.

Overall, I thoroughly enjoyed the people I worked with. One senior sales associate was always dressed to the nines in his pinstriped suit, well-polished shoes, white shirt, dark blue with white polka dot tie, and matching pocket handkerchief. I learned a great deal from him about well-mannered salesmanship. He was the W.C. Fields type though. On occasion when we would "dress up the counters," a young boy would wander through the department. He would whisper to me, "There goes another excuse for birth control."

One evening I was working late and I guess I was tired. As I was organizing the merchandise to make it more presentable and sellable, a reluctant young customer approached me with a belt. I looked down to see that the holes had been punched diagonally from one edge to the other. I couldn't resist a chuckle, and later I wondered if I offended the customer.

When a customer found an item that had a problem or flaw, a markdown on the item was occasionally requested. I always had to consult my supervisor who would determine the discount. So I sent the young fellow, with the belt, to Lew who adjusted the price.

A portion of Lew's salary was commission, but I was hourly. When I had a particularly large sale, I often wondered if I should have given it to Lew. It probably would have helped my relationship with him, but in the department summary, my numbers wouldn't have looked as good. Lew liked my hard work though, so I guess it didn't matter in the long run.

Lew was a great boss and I learned a lot from him. He was caring and a real people-person, but at the same time he was diligent about the appearance of the department and its staff. When I think about Lew I remember a big smile and a lot of hustle.

I was always very quick with the register. There were no scanners or electronic devices, but a large mechanical device with rows of keys marked with various amounts and codes. I could punch those keys faster than almost anyone in the department. I always hated to make the customer wait. Apparently, Lew had suspicions about my ability to ring up a sale so fast so one day he specifically came to watch me as I flew through the keys. He studied me intently and when I was through, just shook his head and walked away. He never said a thing.

Key Points

- Take a moment to allow opportunity to come your way.
- Learn from those that are more experienced.
- Take care of the inventory and make it look good.
- Efficiency can be a blessing to waiting customers.

Columbia Bank and Trust

Sometime in late 1968, upon the recommendation of one of my professors, I had the opportunity to work for the trust department of Columbia Bank and Trust Company. I was still in college working on an accounting degree and appreciated my professor looking out for me. An internship at the bank was a great way to gain experience in a financial institution.

During the school year I worked about twenty hours per week, mostly in the afternoons. When summer came I was asked to work full-time filling in wherever needed. I would send out mailings for a bankrupt insurance company, act as the transfer agent, cancel stock certificates and issue new ones, and any other job that needed to be done. One time they needed someone to show prospective tenants the offices within the facility. So they gave me a master key to the whole building. When I went to return the key to my boss, he said to keep it for the next time I showed an office.

My coworkers were a wonderful bunch. There were the trust officers in their windowed offices who always looked professional whether in suits or dresses. The support staff was equally great to be around however, some were a little more interesting than others. In the accounting posting pool were several larger framed individuals that one officer quietly referred to as the "front four" (as in a pro football team).

I'll never forget a middle-aged woman I worked with. She was always on the lookout for a man. One day she was so excited because she had a luncheon date. When I asked her about it she said, "I was reading the obituaries in the newspaper and saw that a woman had died who was my age. I learned all I could about her from the write-up and then called her widowed husband on the phone. I told him I was an old friend of his wife and wondered if we might meet and reminisce about her. We are meeting over lunch at a local restaurant today."

I could hardly wait for her to come back from lunch to find out if her plan worked. When she returned, I asked if she was successful. She said, "The meal was good, but there was certainly no interest on his part. He did make a pass at the waitress though and is going to take her out."

We used to have weekly meetings where the trust officers would talk about their accounts. One time the following story was told by the assistant department head: "A seventy-year-old sheepherder came in with his twenty-five-year-old girlfriend and said he was going to marry her. He was worth a lot of money and it wasn't long before his children called a meeting saying the wedding had to be stopped because she was nothing more than a gold-digger and would cheat them out of their inheritance. He went ahead, married the girl, and lived another few years.

"After he died and we were settling the estate, the young widow admitted that she had married the old guy for his money. Then she said that she'd really come to love the sweet old fellow during the time they were together." The trust officer said, "Looking back, I think those were the happiest years of his life."

It seemed like every Friday several rough-looking, poorly dressed people came to the department. When I inquired whether we were handing out welfare checks, the response was, "No they are the heirs to some of the estates getting their weekly distribution." It seemed that whether you were rich or poor, you could still be on some form of welfare. It seemed to validate the saying, "Gifts make you a slave."

The Vault

The vault for the trust department was in the basement, right next to the bank vault. The bank vault had about $10,000 in cash at any given time. The trust department vault had about $52 million in negotiable instruments, a lot of which were coupon bonds. In those days, without computer systems, a vault custodian would maintain a file cabinet showing the documentation of who owned which bonds and when the interest was due.

Each day the vault custodian and one other person from the department would take their keys and scissors and head for the vault. The vault custodian would use one key to unlock the outer door, which was a lot like the door to a jail cell. Inside the vault was a large horizontal rotating file that required two keys to open. The two individuals would sit on either side of the file and insert their keys into separate locks, raise the door, and then rotate the file up or down until the appropriate shelf arrived. They would then locate a client's file and pull out the coupon bonds with interest due that day.

The bonds were 18 × 24 inch sheets of paper with an 8 × 10 inch bond certificate in the upper left hand corner. Rows and columns of 1 × 2 inch coupons were attached. The bond had a face amount (usually $1,000), an interest rate, and a maturity date displayed. The company name was prominently displayed along with the type of debenture, and then an elaborate lattice of mesh around the edge with naked Greek and Roman figures centered at the top.

The coupons were dated in intervals every six months or when the interest payment was to be received. One person would locate the appropriate coupon, clip it off, and then return the bond to its file. After clipping a series of coupons for different clients, they would take the coupons to the bank and redeem them for cash to be paid to the trust.

Because of vacation schedules I was asked at various times to serve as the person with the second key or the vault custodian. Late one summer day it hit me; I had the master key to the building, I was substituting for the vault custodian with complete access to the vault, and I previously had access to the second key, which I could have made a copy of. Talk about trust, I had free and open access to $52 million in negotiable bonds. If I were to come in some night I could clean them out, destroy the files, leave town, and it would take months, if not years, to reconstruct the records, if they could. I suppose I should have brought this to someone's attention, but I was young and didn't think they would make the same mistake twice.

I quit shortly before graduation and went to work for the local office of a national CPA firm. About a year later I read in the newspaper that someone had stolen a large sum of money in the form of negotiable bonds from that same trust department. My replacement did exactly what I thought might happen.

Several years later the thief showed up in New York and turned himself in. He said he was tired of running. I reaffirmed that crime never pays, even if it is for a large sum of money.

Internal Controls

The bank building, vaults, office equipment, files, and so forth were the fixed assets required to operate the bank. The inventory was the money and financial instruments (stocks and bonds) that the bank dealt in. Internal controls were violated when I had complete access to everything. No one seemed to think it was a problem when I worked there. Internal controls may be costly, but a company has to weigh the benefit against the cost. Is the benefit of secure assets and inventory worth the cost of more safeguards and systems?

Key Points

- Money makes people do strange things.
- Technology may change processes, but human inclinations and actions are always the same.
- Even money and securities can be inventory.
- Poor internal control over assets can be found in almost any situation.

Frank and Steen
CPA Firm

I worked for the local office of a national CPA firm performing the routine functions of a junior accountant. Major work was found in the tax preparation or audit departments. An audit would usually require interim work (tests of transactions) where the auditors would go to a client and test to see if the systems were working and reliable. At the end of the year the auditors would return to validate the ending balances of the accounts.

Inventory

On one year-end assignment we went to a large warehouse to observe an inventory count. The company sold nuts, bolts, and sundry hardware items. It also sold guns and ammunition, which were kept in a separate locked room with bars on the windows.

Employees were responsible for counting the number of items in each bin and placing a tag with the item identification and count in a prominent place. We would walk around and randomly recount various bins to verify that the information on the tag was correct. I always had the feeling the employees resented us in some way. Perhaps it was my own feeling of self-doubt. It wasn't very exciting work until we discovered a discrepancy that happened occassionally.

At the university we learned about the famous McKesson-Robbins case of the 1930s. Evidently, the president of McKesson decided to add a bogus division and fund it with false revenue and inventory. In those days a physical count of inventory was never taken. When the fraud was discovered, it prompted a change in audit procedures. It became standard practice to verify inventory through a physical count and observation.

Most auditors also validate the count of physical assets by comparing their numbers to a master lists. It is amazing how either the inventory of items to be sold or the office supplies and fixed assets used to facilitate operations can wander off.

Hardware items are easy to count. I was told that counting cattle was much more difficult. They move around a lot while you are trying to count them. Years later when I went to help a cousin brand his cattle, I became very aware of the difficulty of exact numbers. One bright observer said, "Oh, cattle are easy, just count the legs and divide by four."

Accounts Receivable

Another critical function as an auditor was to confirm accounts receivable. This was a process of selecting a few accounts (all the large ones and a random selection of smaller ones) and sending a letter to the payer to confirm the balance as of a certain date. This is an area where businesses can create fictitious accounts receivable that generates bogus revenue for the year.

Sometimes individuals within a company steal money the company receives when it should pay down a receivable. If they are in a position to do so, they will continually apply new money to old accounts, rolling them forward indefinitely. There are so many manipulations that can occur with fixed assets, inventory, receivables, and earnings that accountants and auditors have to be very vigilant.

I left the CPA firm after a few years and took a position with a small service company. I don't think I was cut out to be an auditor or tax accountant.

Key Points

- It is important to have a routine count of inventory.
- It is also important to validate that fixed assets exist and are properly recorded.
- Accounts receivable can be manipulated and must be monitored.
- There are a lot of ways a company can falsify the income statement and report the earnings they desire.

Emerson Advertising Inc.
Part One

History

Two brothers, Dick and Jerry Emerson, were very close and always looked for ways to help each other. Dick eventually became a powerful leader at a major corporation in Omaha, Nebraska, and Jerry offered public relations and advertising services that Dick's corporation needed. Since Dick oversaw all advertising and media for the company and its subsidiaries, he sent all their business to Jerry.

This required Jerry to build a modest company to provide the needed services, but it also presented a potential problem. In any business it is very risky to be dependent on a single dominant client. If Dick was not in a position to send work to Jerry, his company would most certainly fail. To protect against this possibility and to ensure a solid future, Jerry leveraged the base that had been established and attempted to expand with new clients and new markets.

Because Jerry operated a service business, the primary asset was the talent of the employees. To retain the best staff, Jerry initiated an incentive plan that allowed employees to share in the excess earnings of the company through a profit sharing plan. At the end of each year, a certain amount was deposited for each employee in an independent trust, away from the control of Jerry's company.

Also, rather than trying to drum up new clients on his own, Jerry found it easier to acquire companies in other markets that offered the same service to an already established list of clients. Through this process, branch offices were established in several major cities throughout the United States.

Things seemed to go well except for one particular operation. The manager at the Kansas City, Missouri, branch was not a wise financial steward and the operation began to hemorrhage cash to such an extent that the whole network was in trouble.

In 1967, Jerry went to the Emerson offices of a national CPA firm and inquired if there was someone who could provide the expertise needed to clean up the mess. A young CPA, Jonas, seized the opportunity to counsel with Jerry and created a position for himself as the company's new vice president of finance.

Cash is the Key

In solidifying control of the finances of Emerson Advertising Inc. the first move Jonas made was to close the Kansas City office to stop the bleeding.

As Jonas initiated tight financial controls, he became the most powerful person in the company, next to the aging Jerry. He had no direct control over the creative side of the business, supervision of account executives, or soliciting new clients. He found his niche by approving credit for new clients, structuring acquisitions, and "financial engineering."

He soon realized that growth through acquisition required cash, but the cash that was needed from excess earnings was already committed to the employee profit sharing plan. These two principles, growth and sharing excess earnings with employees, were financial enemies.

The acquisition of a new branch office followed a standard pattern. The first step was to find a company within a target market that was somewhat smaller than the head office and relatively successful. Its client list needed to be compatible with the existing network. The owner/manager was contacted to discuss the advantages of the acquisition: a greater network and broader range of services and support. In reality, it was a way for the senior sole proprietor to get value out of the company he had nurtured for many years.

A target price was established, usually one year's gross revenue, and a buyout contract signed. The buyout put an initial chunk of cash into the owner/manager's hands with the rest to be paid over a five-year period, contingent on maintaining the original client-base. This form of buyout required a bucket of cash to make the initial down-payment to the owner/manager.

Working for Emerson

I started working at the Central office of Emerson in 1971. Since it was a service company it had a much lower investment in inventory and fixed assets than a manufacturing entity would have. I soon found that Jonas had instigated a strong cash management system to control the company's delicate financial balance. This required vigilant control of receivables so that cash was not tied up in excessive credit to clients. At the same time, it pushed the limits by delaying accounts payable to secure as much free financing from suppliers and vendors as possible. This relationship, if aggressively managed, could result in facilitating growth as payables exceeded receivables and generated the free financing needed.

Another method to raise cash was to tightly control the actual movement of cash. Relationships with banks in each of the branch office locations were established. All collections of receivables were deposited in those banks and then the money was wired immediately to Emerson's Central office. At the same time, all payments were made from the Central office so that checks for vendor services located in distant cities took several days before they were received, deposited, and cleared the bank. This quick pull of cash and slow push gave the company additional time to use cash.

Often sales executives within the company would find a potential new client that could bring in significant revenues, but they were required to have Jonas approve the deal. The company subscribed to a credit review service called Dun & Bradstreet. Jonas would consult the service to determine whether the potential client had a poor credit rating. If so, they would be denied unless they paid on a cash basis. This made the sales executives furious, but it demonstrated the power Jonas had in attempting to limit bad receivables that could tie up cash for indefinite periods. Another method of reducing the impact of client credit was to sign agreements with larger clients to pay a routine monthly retainer or fee. This would smooth out cash flow to cover monthly payroll and expenses. At the end of the year the accumulated fees would be reconciled against the cost of services provided. Any difference was either charged against or credited to the client. If fee arrangements could not be negotiated, the company pursued an aggressive collection process. In many instances the sales executives themselves ended up being the collection agents. They brought the client in, ran up the expenses, and then had to make sure the receivable was collected in a timely fashion.

On a few occasions old receivables slipped through the cracks and I had to follow up. There was a local amusement park that seemed to be a particular problem. Emerson provided advertising and promotional services to the resort, but the receivable for the resort would remain unpaid as their prime season came to an end, resulting in potential bankruptcy. Ultimately, the resort was acquired by new owners who assumed all prior debts. They signed a long-term note to repay the obligation. This happened three years in a row, yet Emerson continued to take on the resort as a new client with each succeeding owner.

Through this process of instant wire transfers, central distribution of checks, denying potential bad risk clients, aggressive collection of receivables, routine fee arrangements, and delaying payables as long as possible, sufficient cash was available for acquisitions and maintaining the profit sharing plan.

Key Points

- Business is built on powerful connections.
- It is very risky for a business to be dependent on a single dominant client.
- Retaining the best talent may require sharing excess earnings with them.
- Growth and sharing excess earnings with employees are financial enemies.
- Aggressive collection of receivables and delaying payables forces your business partners to finance your company.
- Tightly control the movement of cash every day.
- Don't take on clients with bad credit.
- Smooth cash flow by having clients pay a routine monthly fee.
- Sometimes it is best to have sales associates help collect bad accounts.

Emerson Advertising Inc.
Part two

Company Culture

Jonas was a relatively young man, but was badly balding. He only had a fringe of hair that surrounded his barren pate. One of the most shocking days for the entire company was the day Jonas showed up with his new toupee. It was black and completely covered his deficiency. No one knew exactly how to react to this new development, but we all decided it was best to make no comment.

Jonas was also a very competitive person. Sometime in my third year he decided to initiate a company football pool. There was a large chalk board in the accounting office that served as the betting board. A grid was drawn on the board with National Football League games listed down the left side and betting participants across the top. Each game had the initials of the two competing teams and their point spread.

Points were awarded to the team that was determined to be inferior to make the bet equal. In other words, if the New York Giants (NY) were playing the Dallas Cowboys (Dal) and Dal was favored, then NY might be given six points. This meant that if a participant picked Dal to win and the score was Dal 21 and NY 17, then 6 points would be given to NY and Dal would in fact be a losing bet. Jonas prided himself on being the one to determine the various points to be awarded each game. Around ten employees paid $1 each week to play and the winner received the pot.

This weekly game continued for about two years until one day I encouraged a group of young women working in the accounting office to enter as a team. They each put up 25¢ and would split the winnings, if there were any. The women knew nothing about football and were reluctant to play. I assured them it would be fun; they could compete and I would show them how.

In the newspaper each week was a column by "Jimmy the Greek" who had his own projected point spread. I simply compared the points awarded by Jonas against those by "Jimmy the Greek" and drew up the women's selection. In their first try they won the pool and everyone thought it was real funny that they had stumbled to a win.

The second week they won again. Suddenly the mood of the "informed" contributors changed. No longer was it funny, but something was going on. Jonas finally decided that I was the problem and was somehow helping the girls. He called me to his office and demanded to know how I was selecting the winning teams. I had to reveal my system. From that point on, "Jimmy the Greek" was the official source of point spreads that was used for the pool.

On one occasion I was conducting interviews for a data entry position. We had several applicants, but the one that impressed me the most was a woman with a bachelor's degree from a country in Southeast Asia. I couldn't believe our great luck; we could hire the most qualified candidate and diversify the staff at the same time. So I offered her the job. After she accepted and left, the receptionist told me that her husband filled out the job application. I began to wonder if she could actually read and write English.

She turned out to be a wonderful employee, but the other staff in the department did not accept her into their society. One day she brought a wok in to work and prepared a wonderful lunch for everyone. That broke the ice and she became more comfortable and accepted.

Finding a Better Way

At various times my job was to solve some of the more challenging problems. This was well before desktop or laptop computers. The only computers available were large mainframes where a small company could purchase time. The company purchased an accounting machine to post client charges to ledger cards (one for each client). As the cards were placed in the posting machine to record each charge, a punch paper tape was generated with accumulated data. The tape was supposed to be used in a tape reading machine to generate summary cost reports. The only problem was that Emerson never purchased a tape reader so the tapes and the summary information on them were never used.

I searched the local business district and found a small company that had a machine that would read the tape and produce a series of punch computer cards. We could then take the cards to a mainframe computer and, by use of a program, generate a cost accounting report for each client. The company went years without the ability to generate the report until I took the initiative to solve the problem. Jonas was ecstatic when the reports started coming in and used them extensively.

The system worked great, but the computer had a funny way of truncating some of the data. One client, Farmer's Association, came out as "Farmer's Ass" for the title and made me wonder what other problems the computer was having.

Other Duties

While at Emerson I did basic accounting, posted journal entries, reconciled accounts, generated monthly financial reports, prepared adjusting entries and year-end statements, oversaw treasury functions, prepared payroll and reports, installed an IBM mini computer system, and secured short-term credit from banks.

For several years I prepared the monthly financial statements that were used to monitor how the various branches of the company were doing. This consisted of an individual income statement for each branch detailing all revenues and expenses with a companion column next to the dollar amounts that reflected common sizing. This separate column translated each expense into a percentage of the total revenue. In this way we could quickly see if the salaries and wages category was consistently the same percentage from period to period and at each location.

Accounting for Art

Emerson provided artistic services for some of its clients and therefore employed a staff of artists. Every month as the artists created logos, airbrushed photos, and drafted layouts, they had to fill out time sheets that accounted for every fifteen minutes of every day for which clients would be billed. I'm sure when these artists decided to go into such a creative profession they never imagined they would have to meticulously account for every minute of their time.

At the end of each week the artist would send these time sheets to the accounting department. One of the more interesting things I did was to review the time sheets. Though not my job, it was a labor of love. The sheets would have rows and columns filled in with the appropriate numbers, but all around the edge would be caricatures and sketches of events from the week. After the data from the sheets were posted to the appropriate client, the sheets were filed away. I always thought the sketches were more valuable than the sheets themselves and wondered if I could claim them when they were discarded. I never did.

Rigorous control over people's productive time was emphasized and I'm sure it was irritating for artists to account for every fifteen minutes of their time. Controlling labor costs and making sure they are converted into billable hours that result in revenue is critical. This is how the inventory of people and their work-time translates into earnings for the company.

Employee Stock Ownership Plans

In the mid- to late-seventies, the Federal Government passed the Employee Retirement Income Security Act (ERISA) that allowed companies to initiate employee stock ownership plans (ESOPs). Prior to this, the employee's profit sharing plan had required the company to place in trust excess earnings in their behalf at a bank, which were then invested in blue chip stock such as General Motors (GM), General Electric (GE), and International Business Machines Corporation (IBM).

With the advent of ESOPs, the profit sharing plan could be converted to an employee stock ownership trust which allowed the bank to sell all the blue chip investments and buy stock in the contributing company. As company treasurer, one day I put a stock certificate into my typewriter and typed 29,000 shares. Jonas took the certificate to the bank, which purchased it with the money in trust, and he brought back a wheelbarrow full of cash to Emerson Advertising Inc. The employee's retirement money was now invested in Emerson and their fortunes were dependent on the success of the company. Suddenly, the company had the cash it needed to pursue growth.

In addition to employees owning company stock through the ESOP, the company had a custom where employees could own stock directly. Each year the company would give stock bonuses to valued employees. As treasurer of the company, I was responsible for maintaining the records of who owned how much stock and the issuance of new stock certificates. The senior executives received the greater stock bonuses, with Jonas leading the list. Through the years he amassed a significant share of ownership in the business.

The one downside of having this sudden influx of cash was that it reduced the impetus for strong working capital controls. In Houston, Texas, a new company was acquired every other year, but the fundamental base never seemed to achieve the strength desired. A company would be brought in, but its client list would slowly erode. Perhaps this was the result of poor creative leadership rather than financial controls.

Leaving Emerson

When I left Emerson in 1979 the company's stock was increasing in value each year and the employees were happy. I later heard there were a few years of setbacks where the stock dipped in value and the employees were not as happy. The philosophy was that by owning stock in the company and working for the company, the employees controlled their own financial destiny. This was a bit of a hollow promise since the ESOP controlled the majority of the stock. When it came time for the owners of the stock to vote on company directors and officers, the officers voted for themselves with the shares held by the ESOP.

Accounting Management Styles

The downside of having a CPA running things is that they are not typically creative or nurturing. One time Emerson had the opportunity to pitch their services to a national client. During the presentation Jonas talked about how inexpensively the company could provide its services since people in the state were paid less than the national average. The emphasis should have been on how effective we were and not on how cheap. We did not land the client.

Many times employees in the accounting and finance departments complained that Jonas had a philosophy of "hire 'em, tire 'em, and fire 'em." He exploited staff instead of helping to develop their skills. Years after I left, I occasionally ran into Doug, a fellow who worked for Jonas. He talked about the great opportunities that were promised to him if he worked hard. I told him to work hard, but knew from personal experience that Jonas could not be trusted.

One night Doug called me at home. I didn't understand why, but then he indicated he had been passed over for a promised promotion. I consoled him as best I could and told him there was life after Emerson. Later, I learned that the day after we talked he took his own life, leaving a wife and children behind.

A few years after I left Emerson, Jonas was promoted to chief executive officer (CEO). He had amassed a sizable portion of stock and within a few years sold the company and took his profits. This has always been my concern about small regional markets: they merely grow companies to be sold to the highest bidder. Their corporate center functions are moved to larger cities, the developers take their profits, and the result is a city full of processing centers. The real interesting jobs are relocated somewhere else. With no corporate jobs left, the only hope for future generations is to build their own entity to be sold off in the next round.

Key Points

- Many successful business people are competitive and can be egotistical.
- Office pools can offer opportunity for esprit de corps—unless you make your boss look bad.
- Cultural integration may require a fair amount of patience.
- A little initiative can overcome the most troubling problem. Sometimes it requires thinking outside the box.
- Common-size financial statements are a quick way to spot deviations from the norm.
- Accounting can be a tedious process—even for the most creative types.
- Government actions can change the game at any time.
- Using the employee's retirement cash can significantly aid company growth prospects.

- Clients want to know how good you are, not how cheap.
- When it comes to promised promotions, a bird in the hand is worth two in the bush.
- Entrepreneurs grow firms in small markets to be sold to major corporations for quick profits.

Family Healthcare Inc.
Part One

Even with a master of business administration
(MBA), a Certified Public Accountant license,
and significant corporate experience, finding
another job that would offer unlimited upward
opportunity seemed a challenge at the time. My
brother learned in one of his MBA classes that a
large, private corporation was hiring for their
Internal Audit department. I applied and was
hired.

Family Healthcare Inc. History

Family Healthcare Inc. (FHC) was formed in
1975 when a group of decentralized providers of
health services were brought together under a new
central corporate organization. This simple
statement doesn't even begin to describe the
major trauma associated with such a cultural shift.
When antonymous entities are asked to become
part of a centralized system, the lines of battle are
quickly drawn where turf and terrain may appear
civil, but in reality are subtle war zones.
Negotiating and positioning continued from 1979
to 1989, the ten years I worked there.

Sherman, the new CEO of Family Healthcare,
proceeded to fill the various vice presidential
positions in the corporate office. A key position
was vice president of finance/chief financial
officer (CFO). He asked one of the large national
CPA firms that had healthcare experience to help
define the role of CFO. They sent Braxton, a

young 30-year-old CPA from one of the major offices in the country. As Braxton consulted with Sherman, he defined the person that was needed for the position as someone almost exactly like himself; he was ultimately hired for the job. Afterwards an internal auditing staff was hired and that's where I came in.

Internal Auditor

In 1979, after seven years, I left the position of treasurer at Emerson Advertising Inc. and accepted an internal auditor position with Family Healthcare Inc. At my previous employer I had not only prepared financial statements and worked in most aspects of accounting and finance, but I had written computer programs for use at an external service bureau and installed an internal computer system.

As an internal auditor at FHC I was assigned to a multitude of tasks, but a few that stand out were: (1) trying to uncover lost charges, (2) review processes for the collection of accounts receivable, and (3) lost inventory. Lost charges came about when procedures were performed in various hospitals but no charge was ever made in the accounting records. It seemed the inventory of supplies could not be controlled and were constantly disappearing.

For example, my neighbor was a medical student at a major university. One day I received a minor injury that my neighbor became aware of. He was excited to demonstrate what he had learned and quickly drove me to the university's hospital. We entered through the service entrance and went to one of the treatment areas. He did a fine job of addressing my need and we left. That was it. There was no paperwork or record indicating that the facility or supplies were used. When I raised the issue, his response was that it was simply not a problem.

On another occasion I was in a meeting with one of the vice presidents of FHC. We began talking about how the latest fashion trend was for high school and college students to wear a particular type of healthcare uniform we had in inventory. We complained about losing uniforms, and how it was driving up costs. Suddenly, the vice president got a sheepish look on his face and admitted that his son was somehow acquiring the garments and wearing them.

Accounts Receivable Collections

Another concern to auditors was the loss of cash receipts that resulted from revenue that was never collected. As I travelled to various subsidiaries, it became apparent that each entity handled the collection of accounts receivable through a similar process, but with subtle differences that would result in varying degrees of divergent success.

The major problem was the attention given to old receivable, those that were uncollected for long periods of time. Some collection personnel would put these in special places, like bottom drawers, and occasionally review them. They frequently became lost or forgotten about and would become totally uncollectable.

As auditors, we constantly tried to reinforce a solid system of internal controls that removed any possibility of loss, theft, or fraud.

Looking for a Better Way

I worked for a year as a staff auditor and gained valuable experience, but found the job less than satisfying. As the first summer approached, Peter, my supervisor, was concerned about whether there would be enough work to keep the staff of three auditors busy and out of trouble. He had the external computer service bureau print the general ledger for all departments in Family Healthcare's twenty entities. The printout was almost 2 feet thick. Peter had the monster placed on a desk in the audit area with the following instructions: "Go through all the accounts and find variances in either account title or number. For example, all cash accounts should have the same name and number."

Looking at the tedious work involved, I decided that it was not how I was going to spend my summer. I asked him, "Where did you get that printout?"

Peter said, "I got it from the Services Bureau where the general ledger is maintained on a magnetic tape."

It was in fact the same service bureau where I had run some of Emerson's reports. I asked Peter if I could go over and generate a report from the general ledger.

He said, "No, they wouldn't allow that. You could corrupt the general ledger and we would lose data."

I then asked, "What if they made a copy of the general ledger on another tape and allowed me access to that?"

He continued to throw up roadblocks about why it was not possible, but I had an answer for every one of them. Finally, I wore him down and was given access to a copy of the magnetic tape. I went to the service bureau, had them tell me the format of the general ledger file, found a programming book in the user's area for a simple report-writer, punched some computer cards, and submitted the program. It took a few days of trial and error, but eventually I was able to sort the file by account, subsidiary, and department instead of by subsidiary, department, and account. When the report was done I took another 2 foot tall printout to the corporate offices, placed it on Peter's desk, and said, "The job is done."

I think I frustrated his plan to keep the staff busy all summer. It wasn't that I was trying to be difficult; I just knew there had to be a better way. I was determined to find it using the tools at my disposal.

Key Points

- Consultants are in a great position to create high-powered job opportunities at a corporation.

- Changing corporate culture requires a great deal of patience (yes, I'll say it once again).
- It was difficult to control the inventory of supplies that were constantly disappearing.
- Auditors were concerned about the loss of cash receipts that resulted from revenue that was never collected.
- Sometimes there is a better way of doing things by utilizing the tools at your disposal.

Healthcare Inc.
Part Two

In a few days I received a call from Stanley, the director of budgeting and governmental compliance for Family Healthcare. He heard about my success with the general ledger and wanted to take me to lunch. Over lunch he asked if I was happy in auditing and whether I would consider transferring to budgeting. He offered me a substantial raise, I accepted, and was named budget manager for the entire corporation. In auditing, I was looking for a better way and not a promotion, but I was glad it happened.

It soon became evident as I developed standardized processes and procedures for the corporation that centralizing a historically decentralized organization was not going to be easy. Changing corporate culture is extremely difficult. Every time I created what I thought would be a wonderfully standardized form for reporting statistics or data, it seemed the personnel at the various subsidiaries would stay up all night trying to frustrate the system and circumvent compliance.

The Strategic/Budgeting Planning Process

Strategic planning and budgeting was a year-long process and involved almost the entire company. This process was critical to the company because it followed the long standing wisdom of (1) assess where you are, (2) set goals for the future, (3) implement plans to reach those goals, and (4) reevaluate how you are doing.

The title of this work is *FIRE and Other Stuff*, where the emphasis is on financial controls. However, these controls are meaningless without the broader strategic direction of the company. At the same time, strategic planning is useless without the insurance that financial controls bring.

The strategic planning and budgeting process began in December with brainstorming sessions and wish list proposals. During the brainstorming phase, all stakeholders had the opportunity to present their wish lists or ideas about how they envisioned their department, subsidiary, or the corporation. They would talk about new products and services, technological changes on the horizon, reconfiguring existing facilities, and major changes in personnel and staffing. In most cases the ideas were not original to them, but reflected a "keeping up with the Joneses" mentality as they read through professional journals, or what I would call the "Christmas Wish Book."

On one occasion, Family Healthcare's largest subsidiary suggested a form of "new technology." I received a call about how they had an original idea for creating growth in kidney stone treatment. It was called a Lithotripter.

Apparently shock waves had shattered ice crystals on an airplane once. This inspired someone to translate the phenomenon for use in the medical field. A company in Germany focused shock waves to pulverize kidney stones. It would cost $1 million for the subsidiary to purchase the device and build a soundproof room to house it.

When they first presented the idea, the brochure from the German company pictured an attractive young blond woman wearing a bathing suit in a tub of water. A large pointed device was focused at her. The ad was designed to show how the device would be used and its benefits.

Healthcare economists knew the cost for the traditional medical treatment for kidney stones, but they had no idea how to price the new procedure. It had the potential to radically change the delivery of that service in the market.

The idea floated around the corporation for a year before it was approved as a special exception to the budget. Construction went forward with a projection of 2,000 procedures the first year. By the end of that year the count was well ahead of the expected number. Volume, revenue, and income jumped the second year. It appeared like this was going to be a great investment in fixed assets.

During the third year the German company introduced a second-generation portable Lithotripter. Twenty-three physicians in the local market joined forces, purchased the new Lithostar, put it in a semi-truck, and hauled it from place to place. The volume for our lithotripter suddenly evaporated.

This is just one example of why a company needs to be careful when investing in fixed assets. Wise choices can provide great gains and advantage in the marketplace. Poor choices result in financial loss that wastes resources, don't meet customer needs, and ultimately kill the enterprise.

Strategic business planning sessions were held in January. The heads of each subsidiary developed a base-case set of financials projecting the next three year's revenues, expenses, and earnings. This base case assumed there would be no changes in services or investment in new fixed assets. With the lack of new products and services, there would likely be some deterioration of market share and earnings.

Wish list items would be quantified as to asset needs, effect on the balance sheet, and related operating impacts. Next, a new financial projection was generated showing a scenario where the base case incorporated all the proposed changes for the next three years. In other words, if approval was given to proceed with the acquisition of the list of proposed fixed assets, there could be additional market share, more revenue and prosperity for the company.

As far as the Lithotripter, the base case without the new technology would reflect a slow deterioration of revenue. A total case would show a layer of new revenue as a result of the Lithotripter being added to the base case as well as continued growth in overall revenue.

Global metrics were established in February. All of the business plans were merged into a unified corporate roll-up. This roll-up revealed how much money was needed to fund the purchase of fixed assets that supported new ideas.

At the same time, consolidated financials showed how much cash would be available from operations to pay for projects and what kind of a bottom-line target was required to generate the cash. There was always more demand for money to fund projects than cash generated from operations. Spending targets would be cut and earnings targets increased. If we did everything everyone wanted we would need $50 million. But, we only had a proposed 5% profit margin generating less than $25 million. If we reduced the consolidated spending to $40 million and increased the earnings target to 7%, we could remain in balance. These became the two global metrics.

The corporate office then distributed target metrics to each subsidiary specifying a maximum amount that could be spent for capital budget (asset acquisitions) and a minimum profit margin target for operating budget (cash generated). More specifically, a subsidiary would be told they had no more than $2 million to budget for new assets and must generate a minimum 6% bottom line.

The limits on expenditures for fixed assets created some unusual problems. In several situations a subsidiary would lease equipment rather than purchase it to get around the capital budgeting restrictions. One year the corporation found that a subsidiary had so much leased equipment that the leasing company was storing its idle machinery in the basement of the hospital.

When I did an analysis, I found the subsidiary was paying more to lease one machine for one year that it would cost to purchase it. The response from the subsidiary's management team was, "You wouldn't let us buy it, we needed it, and the only other option was to lease it." A special exemption beyond the budget was granted to allow the subsidiary to purchase everything they had leased.

The bottom line was usually not affected by the decision to lease versus purchase. Lease expense was sometimes equal to the depreciation expense on the income statement. While earnings would be the same in either case, depreciation was a non-cash entry and so leasing resulted in a lower operating cash flow. Do you pay now through acquisition or pay as you go through leasing? Usually, leasing was more expensive.

From March through April, after global metrics (capital spending targets and profit margins) were established, each subsidiary would begin the process of screening capital budget (new asset) proposals. As budget manager, I developed a standardized set of forms and a review process to determine justification of need, the initial investment required, projected operating cash flows for up to ten years, and the related net present value (NPV) and benefit cost ratio (BCR) for each project. While determining which ideas should be approved, projects would be ranked and reviewed.

For the three years I served as corporate budget manager, I personally reviewed every project proposed. Hundreds of projects were ranked according to those that offered the greatest benefit relative to cost. For projects with no revenue stream, it was necessary to determine the greatest need. We followed the same process that had been developed at General Motors years before:

General Motors' Capital Budgeting Process in the 1920s

"The core of our concept lay in the determination of the propriety of proposed projects. Four principles were to be satisfied, which were stated as follows:

1. Is the Project a logical or necessary one considered as a commercial venture?
2. Has the Project been properly developed technically?
3. Is the Project proper, considering the interest of the Corporation as a whole?
4. What is the relative value of the Project to the Corporation as compared with other Projects under consideration, from the standpoint not only of the return on the necessary capital to be invested, but of the need of the particular Project in supporting the operations of the corporation as a whole?"[1]

---

[1] Sloan, Alfred P., *My Years With General Motors* (MacFadden-Bartell Book, New York, 1965) page 120.

It was thought that technological change would reduce cost, but it rarely, if ever, did. Innovation usually resulted in a bigger market with greater service and more possibilities but not necessarily lower costs.

Staffing standards were established in June. After the capital budgeting and review seasons were complete, the major work on the operating budget (projected income statement) began. I would pull together projected inflation percentages for various expense items and send those to each subsidiary. In addition, I would work closely with a group of management engineers who would set staffing standards for almost every department at each hospital.

These standards would include a fixed and variable staffing component that established how many people a department could employ based on their projected volume. Long hard battles were sometimes fought over whether these numbers were optimal, achievable, or realistic. I worked closely with the marketing and planning staff to determine realistic volume projections.

My boss and I went to an operating budget review at a large hospital where the chief operating officer proudly announced they had cut next year's budget for salaries and wages by 5%. That seemed like a wonderful achievement until I looked at the numbers and saw that they were adding 100 people to the payroll beyond the current year's staffing.

I asked, "How can you cut salaries by 5% and add 100 people?" They said they were currently operating below staffing standards as set by management engineering because they couldn't find qualified employees. I asked if they were getting the job done and was assured that quality was not suffering.

The obvious problem was that the hospital was gaming the system. By driving the standards up, they could come in under what was expected and still increase staffing beyond where they were currently operating.

From July through September an operating budget was developed. Working within corporate established metrics and their own historic experience, each hospital would incorporate all relevant data and generate an operating budget that met or exceeded the global earnings target. This would be a summary of all individual department budgets. Some departments only had maintenance or business office expenses. Departments with revenues and expenses were called profit centers because they directly charged for a service, incurred expenses, and recognized a net income.

Besides staffing standards, another major battle revolved around the discussion of corporate office allocation. Since the corporate office generated no revenue on its own, the expenses for these centralized support functions had to be absorbed by each subsidiary and a method of allocation devised to spread these costs to each entity. This generally caused some resentment at the subsidiary level as they witnessed corporate costs increase without any control on their part.

Expense departments simply added the increased charge. Profit departments had to increase revenue enough to cover their own expenses plus the allocation for administrative areas. For example, the laboratory might have department expenses of $1 million and add expenses of $200K for uncontrollable administrative charges. They always complained about having to set their revenue high enough to cover both.

Reviews and modifications were made in October. The budgeting game was always a give and take process with sufficient pad incorporated to weather the various cuts that higher levels of management made to justify their existence. Regional management made cuts, corporate management made cuts, and of course the board's finance committee felt it was their duty to make adjustments.

One year we completed reviews at all levels, except for the board's finance committee. They came back and wanted one of our major hospitals to cut their expenses to achieve a higher bottom-line. I conveyed the message to hospital management and received the following response: "We think our initial projection of volume was too low, so if we increase our volume and related revenue, we can get to the number you want without cutting expenses."

Department budget (November to December)
Department budgets were finalized from November to December. Once budgets were

approved at the board level, final numbers were sent back to the subsidiaries to be spread over each of the twelve months of the budget year. It was always a challenge to get the subsidiaries to allocate the data on a seasonal basis rather than dividing by twelve.

When all this was done, the target year would begin and actual performance would be compared against budget every month. It was good when actual revenues were higher than budget. It was bad when actual expenses exceeded budget. Each subsidiary had to prepare a twentieth-of-the-month report to explain major variances from the previous month's budget.

Management hated having to justify variances from budget. They would come up with the most interesting responses to expense overages. In many cases I would compare reports from several subsidiaries and see an overage in salaries. I would read various explanations for the excesses from all of my reporting hospitals, all of them different: unusually high vacation, too much training time, or the budget was wrong. I wanted to scream when I heard that last excuse. They developed the budget and now were saying it was wrong.

Finally, I read a report that said there was a computer problem where the corporation allocation method arbitrarily put a couple extra days of pay into the wrong month. This affected all subsidiaries and after adjusting for that, every other excuse appeared ridiculous. Determining the real reason for budget variances became an art that, after much experience, I felt I had a pretty good handle on.

The Process

To summarize, the planning and budgeting process took one year to complete

1. Brainstorming and Wish Lists (December)
2. Strategic Business Plan (January)
3. Establishing Global Metrics (February)
4. Capital Budgeting (March through April)
5. Establish Staffing Standards (June)
6. Operating Budgeting (July to September)
7. Review and Modifications (October)
8. Department Budget (November to December)
9. Performance Reporting (January to December)

Managing Accounts Receivable

For the three years I worked as budget manager in the corporate office I oversaw the budgeting process. It was an extremely rewarding time where I was able to view the entire strategic landscape of a billion dollar corporation.

About the time I moved from internal auditing to budget manager, the corporation was making a concerted effort to standardize and centralize most accounts receivable management functions. The corporation set up their own collection agency and hired a man named Clyde to run it. He quickly expanded an operation that had been just a few people into an agency of about 100.

Clyde required all subsidiaries to issue the first bill within five days of service, with a follow-up by the end of the first month. If the bill was not paid within a specified period it was immediately turned over to the Central Collection Agency. If the bill was not collected, a more intensive follow-up began: attorneys sending collection letters, etc. Clyde's right-hand man was his brother, an attorney, who profited significantly from all the new work. Nevertheless, it was an aggressive accounts receivable collection system that seemed to be highly effective.

It was Family Healthcare's policy that each subsidiary had to maintain its own board of directors. I'll never forget when a new subsidiary was acquired and the old board of directors had to be told they no longer needed to review each account receivable at every board meeting.

Key Points

- I was looking for a better way and not a promotion, but I was glad it came.
- Changing corporate culture is extremely difficult.
- Strategic planning is useless without the assurance financial controls bring.
- Poor choices result in financial loss that waste resources, don't meet customer needs, and ultimately kill the enterprise.

- With a lack of new products and services there would generally be some deterioration of market share and earnings.
- If we reduced the consolidated spending to $40 million and increased the earnings target to 7%, we could remain in balance. These became the two global metrics.
- A subsidiary would lease equipment rather than purchase it to get around capital budgeting restrictions.
- It was assumed that technological change would ultimately reduce cost, but it rarely, if ever, did.
- One obvious problem was that a subsidiary would attempt to game the system and drive standards up.
- The budgeting game was always a give and take process with sufficient pad incorporated to weather the various cuts that higher levels of management would make to justify their existence.
- Determining the real reason for budget variances became an art that, after much experience, I felt I had a pretty good handle on.

Family Healthcare Inc.
Part Three

Regional Director of Finance

I served as budget manager until 1983. At that time it was determined that a new level of management, the regional level, was needed. Three regions (North, Central, and Southern) were formed with Manuel as the vice president of the central region, which happened to be the largest. Each region would have a financial and planning officer. Manuel approached me and asked if I was interested in being the CFO of the Central Region; I accepted. It may seem strange to move from a broad corporate position to a regional position, but the new position had the title of director instead of manager. It also had more perks and direct responsibility for actual financial operations, in addition to budgeting.

As regional CFO I would shepherd each subsidiary in my region through the budgeting process as I supported Manuel and our director of planning and marketing through the strategic planning process. It was curious how we could never get everyone to understand how strategic planning worked. Every year the subsidiaries would bring in their list of new strategies and there would be a debate over whether they were indeed strategies or simply action plans. To this day I'm still not sure what the difference is between the two. But evidently someone knows, at least I think they do.

Family Healthcare Inc.
Seymour, chief executive officer
Braxton, chief financial officer

Medical Delivery Division
Dudley, chief executive officer
Ernest, chief financial officer

Central Region
Manuel, chief operating officer
Me, chief financial officer
Various Subsidiaries
A chief executive office for each
A chief financial officer for each

Once the planning process was complete we went into operation mode. Every month we had a review session where Manuel and I would meet with Dudley, the president of our division, and Ernest, the divisional CFO. I prepared the twentieth-of-the-month report that explained how each subsidiary performed compared to budget. I've often explained it as a session where pleasantries were exchanged between administrators for a few moments, and then for the next hour the divisional CFO would take out his whip and beat me over every major variance from budget.

When a significant variance was discovered, it was always followed by two questions: "Is this a one month aberration, a carry-over from a prior month, or a carry-over to the next month?" And, "Will this variance continue through the year?"

The essence was to determine what the cumulative total-year impact would be and what kind of corrective action was needed. We're talking about year-end earnings.

Monthly Bottom-Line Targets

I had a dotted-line reporting relationship with Ernest who recently became vice president of finance or CFO. Soon after that the controller for one of my subsidiaries called and said his volume was down for the month and wondered what the goal was. I asked what he meant. "Well, I can meet the bottom-line percentage of revenue, but I don't think I can make the budgeted dollar amount." He asked if the goal was the net income percentage or the net income dollars. I wanted to be in concert with my boss, so I asked Manuel what he understood the goal to be. He said it was the percentage, so I felt we were within the targeted limits.

At the next monthly review meeting Ernest asked what was wrong with that particular subsidiary. I was pleased to announce that volume was down, but that we were able to achieve the necessary net income percentage. Ernest exploded and lectured me about how I did not understand. He argued that the goal was the net income dollars. I looked at Manuel for support, but didn't seem to get any. I was on my own. I said to Ernest, "Let me get this straight. No matter what the volume does, the goal is to meet the bottom-line dollars."

"No, no," he said. "If the volume is down the goal is the dollars. If the volume is up the goal is the percentage. As a minimum, the corporation must always have those dollars because we have interest payments due and must always have dollars to pay those commitments."

Cookie Jar Accounting

The first year Ernest was on board we were approaching year-end and it had been a good year. We had budgeted a $5 million bottom-line, but the actual was coming in at $15 million. One day Ernest came into my office and announced that corporate accounting for allowance for doubtful accounts was so poor that he was going to adjust it upward until it could be clearly analyzed. He laid out a schedule of journal entries, one for each of my subsidiaries that needed to be posted before year-end. The entries effectively increased bad debt expense on the income statement, at each unit, with a corresponding adjustment to the accounts receivable on the balance sheet. It wasn't until later that I learned this was classic cookie jar accounting: taking earnings out of a good year and holding them back on the balance sheet until needed in a future year.

After the journal entries were posted, the actual performance for the year was $6 million, just slightly better than the budgeted $5 million. Everyone on the management team received their bonuses and all were happy. The auditors certainly didn't complain, because we were simply being conservative.

The next year-end things were looking good until December when, for some reason, the bottom fell out. The actual for the year was going to end up $2 million under budget. All heck broke loose. Not only were we hurting the current-year bonuses for management, but the five-year bonus plan for senior management was in danger.

Ernest produced schedules showing that our allowance for doubtful accounts adjustment had been too aggressive in the prior year and could be reduced in the current year. Entries were made to reduce bad debt expense and increase the bottom-line by a sufficient amount to raise the actual net income just above the budgeted net income. Ernest was a hero and began a slow and methodical move to increase his power within the company.

Interest Rate Problems

One of the subsidiaries in our region was to undergo a major renovation that would require $100 million for a new building. The financing for this was to come from selling 30-year bonds through an underwriter in New York. Unfortunately, during that time interest rates were higher than they had been in recent history. They were approximately 16% in 1983. The corporation had expected to pay about 8% on $100 million or $8 million per year. The higher rate could have added another $8 million per year to our interest expense.

Some of the corporate officers came back from their trip to New York and announced they were continuing the borrowing process but not with 30-year bonds. Instead they would sell seven-day commercial paper paying 8% interest. This would require rolling the paper over every week until long-term interest rates fell, and then 30-year bonds would be issued. We secured the financing and built the new facility. This was the ultimate fixed asset purchase.

The Ultimate Strategy

The corporation determined that expansion was their ultimate strategy. They brought George, a CEO from one of the subsidiaries, to the corporate office and charged him with the task of identifying potential targets for acquisition. His office was right next to mine and on occasion I would poke my head in his office to see how things were going. He had a large map of the United States with about a hundred pushpins in various locations throughout the Central states.

That summer the corporation contracted with McKinsey & Company of New York to determine whether our global corporate strategy was on target. A few people were sequestered in some open space on an upper floor of our corporate office all summer.

At the end of their engagement McKinsey & Company presented their report to the management team and the board. It included many recommendations, but the most critical was that acquiring additional health service providers (clinics and hospitals) all across the country was not the best option. The better approach would be for Family Healthcare Inc. to focus on regional centers and integrate vertically, acquiring suppliers and purchasing physician practices within the existing established geographic area.

Within days of the report, George and his map of the United States were gone and the office was vacant.

Basic Principles

Since we are talking about ultimate strategies, let me divert one moment. One day in Manual's office he handed me an $8\frac{1}{2} \times 11$ inch paper with a typed message. I read it, asked if I could make a copy of it, and have kept it ever since as part of my personal resources. It has been changed slightly, but this is the essence of what it said:

When your life is over and you look back, what are the things that will bring the most happiness and fulfillment? Let me tell you what they are:

1. You must account for who you are. Have you been patient with yourself and taken every opportunity to enlarge your own personal set of talents? Have you grown into being the best person that you could be in doing good?

2. Have you been actively engaged in making your spouse happy, ensuring his/her needs have been met as an individual, and they have been able to maximize their talents? Have you been patient with them?

3. Have you nurtured each of your children individually? Have you done everything in your power to let them grow into who they want to be and not what you want them to be? Have you been

patient with them?

4. Have you been of service to your fellow man? Have you loved those with whom you deal most closely? Have you patiently forgiven those that may have committed an error toward you?

5. Have you contributed in a positive manner to your community, state, country, and the world?

6. Have you been honest in your dealings with others?

This compilation may seem out of place as I reflect on my business dealings. It is more significant than one might think. Solon, the great merchant who saved Athens from class warfare in 600 BCE, is one of my heroes. He was called the great lawgiver and ruled for about ten years.

When he completed his service he travelled extensively throughout the known world. When he arrived at the court of Croesus, the wealthiest man in the world, Solon was asked to name the happiest man he ever met. Croesus was fishing for a compliment. Solon responded with the name of a citizen of Athens who employed principles much like those outlined above. The story gets better from there.

Aesop the Greek teller of fables was in attendance at the court. After witnessing what Solon did, he pulled him aside and counseled that "one should avoid meeting with powerful people, but if it is necessary, they should be told what they want to hear."

Solon told Aesop that he was only half correct. "One should avoid meeting with powerful people, but if it is necessary, they should be told what they must know."

Sometime later Croesus and his army were defeated by Cyrus the Great. Croesus was put to the stake to be burned. As they were binding him he exclaimed, "Solon, Solon, Solon!" Cyrus said, "Who is this God you pray to?"

Croesus related what he had been told by Solon. Cyrus thought it was so brilliant that he released Croesus and let him live. It is said that one ruler was saved and another was taught through Solon's wisdom.

Budgeting Games

I always tried to meet my goals and felt very successful, but it soon became obvious that there was a broader game to be played. One year as we went through the budgeting process the corporate goal was outlined as a consolidated 6% bottom line, or close to that. Our region came in exactly on target after a very rigorous process. The Northern Region came in well below their target and complained about the major challenges they faced.

The Southern Region exceeded their goal because they were determined to show the way and be exemplary team players. Ernest came to me and said, "I need more out of your region. You are the largest, and both of the other regions have more challenges than you do."

By the end of that year my region met our targets with a small margin. The Northern Region, apparently stricken with major challenges, completely turned things around and were well over budget. They were also praised for their heroic efforts.

The Southern Region, who was such a team player to begin with, was well below their goal, explaining that circumstances beyond their control had created one of the most difficult years ever. Ernest praised the other regions for working so hard that year, but said that the Central Region had cruised along with easy goals. I felt like saying, "Sometimes what looks easy is the result of monumental effort and not gamesmanship."

Strategic Artistry

We would often hold high-level meetings in the executive conference room. On one occasion we went into the opulently appointed room to find the company had purchased a new mobile white board.

During the course of our strategic planning meeting they asked me to record on the board our ideas. I went to the board, picked up the only marker on the tray, and began to draft a beautiful outline of our grandest proposals.

I filled the whole board while another person in the room took notes for later dissemination. It was one of the best planning session we ever had. When we were finished I went to erase the board and found that the marker I used was a permanent marker, not a dry erase marker.

That wasn't the biggest problem. The board was a brand new technology that worked like a SMART Board. It automatically generated a computer document from what was written on the surface. It was a very expensive technology for its time and I had just destroyed it.

The Hiring Process

On one occasion I needed to hire an assistant to help with financial analysis. Before selecting one of two final candidates, I asked another financial executive to conduct a round of interviews. At the end of those interviews I learned the executive posed the following question to each person: "Can you define WACC?"

One of the candidates was quick to respond with the correct answer: "WACC stands for the weighted average cost of capital and is the cost of external funding for the company weighted by the proportion those funds represent of the total." The other candidate was completely caught off guard and unable to give a satisfactory answer to the question. I determined that if I ever taught finance, I would make sure my students could answer that question.

A Management Lesson

At Family Healthcare I had two supervisors. I had a solid line reporting relationship with Manuel, vice president for operations for the Central Region, and a dotted line to Ernest, corporate vice president of finance. The VP of operations was an organized manager, had a master's degree in management, and did a great job. The VP of finance came from one of the large CPA firms and had a "damn it, do it" kind of attitude.

It was the end of 1984. We had a new controller at one hospital, Alexander. The external auditing firm would usually perform two engagements to audit the books. They would come into a subsidiary for a period of time, review how the systems worked, and determine whether they could be relied upon. Then they would come back at the end of the year, and depending on how the interim work went, they would validate the final numbers.

I received a call from Ernest who said that the interim work at Alexander's hospital did not go well. It appeared year-end work would be a mess. Because of Family Healthcare's size, there was a very short window for that hospital's audit. If it had to be extended the whole audit would be late going to the board of directors. The message was loud and clear: take care of it.

I drove out to visit with Alexander. I told him what the external auditors had reported to the corporate office. I also indicated that everyone was looking at the year-end work, and if things were not in good shape when the auditors came, we would both be in trouble. We were in this together and I asked if he needed help getting ready for year-end. He appreciated my support, but said that he would take care of it and guaranteed there would not be a problem. I once again offered to provide support in terms of getting other people to come in and help, but he said I didn't need to worry.

I checked with him periodically and found that the accounting staff was putting in the time required to address matters. He really seemed to respond to a collaborative atmosphere as opposed to an adversarial approach. When the auditors finished the audit, they praised Alexander's group for being ready on time and in great shape.

Profound Management Wisdom

One day I went into another executive's office and we discussed motivation. He was a retired military man that I had great respect for. At that time he said what I feel is one of the most profound things I ever heard. He said, "If you drive an army, they will do the job with some reluctance. But, if in their hearts they have a desire to achieve the goal, get out of their way."

Key Points

- Most people do not understand the difference between a strategy and a tactic.
- People must be held accountable for their area of responsibility.
- You must determine what the total-year impact from a budget variance will be and what corrective action is required.
- Irrespective of sales volume, you must have the funds available to pay for interest expense when it is due.

- Every good executive accountant prides themself on knowing how to employ techniques like cookie jar accounting to smooth the earnings from year-to-year.
- Your job may totally depend on the strategic direction a company takes.
- In the middle of corporate economics, never lose sight of personal goals.
- Telling the truth in the short-term may be a bad tactic. In the end it may save the whole entity.
- Gamesmanship is constantly at play in corporate politics.
- People respond heroically to supportive leadership.
- "If you drive an army, they will do the job with some reluctance. But, if in their hearts they have a desire to achieve the goal, get out of their way."

Healthcare Inc.
Part Four

Buying Assets

The largest hospital in the Central Region supported several Doc-in-a-Box facilities in their market. These clinics provided urgent care services in various communities. To break-even, we determined that each unit had to serve at least 30 patients per day. Only two of these were ever in the black, most being in the red.

One day I received a call from the CFO of the hospital. He said that a corporation who ran nine similar urgent care facilities was leaving the market and put all nine clinics up for sale. The subsidiary was only interested in one of the nine and was proposing that we move quickly to purchase it.

I told them to prepare the required paperwork, and if I agreed with the proposal, would proceed to the next step. On my way to visit the clinic, I was convinced it was in a decent location and had possibilities. When the projections came in, it was curious to see exactly thirty sales per day were forecast. Checking the historical record, the entity had never served more than twenty per day. I challenged the CFO who replied: "We think by putting our name on the building, our brand will easily attract the requisite numbers."

I was sure he was blowing smoke, but understood the nature of clinics. When I took the proposal to Ernest, he hit the roof: "How can you bring this thing to me? The numbers don't make sense. Would you purchase this thing?"

I said, "As for myself, I'd never buy it. But these centers are loss leader entry points to the hospital. They are a critical part of the network, and this one is in a market where we have no exposure. You have to look at not only the revenues generated by this single entity, but the effect it will have on the hospital and its network."

He fought the proposal through the entire process, but it eventually was approved. I never followed up to see what the average volume per day was, but trusted that it was beneficial for the system.

Breakeven Experience

While director of finance for the Central Region I oversaw the financial operations of four of the largest hospitals. It was during this time that corporate planners determined there would be an opportunity to build a freestanding psychiatric hospital within my region.

The new facility opened and operated for a portion of 1986 under the direction of the corporate office. Toward the end of 1986 I was notified that I would be responsible for the financial operations of the new hospital and it would be included in my region for 1987. When I looked at the budget for 1987, the subsidiary was targeted to lose $1 million. I became concerned because I knew I would be continually hammered over the next year for an operation that did not make money. With monthly accountability reporting in mind, I realized that even with the $1 million budgeted loss, there would be constant pressure to work toward no loss at all.

At the end of January 1987, the new subsidiary lost $200K for the month. A quick calculation suggested that if that performance continued we could lose $2.4 million for the year. I did a detailed analysis of the entity's financial statements and found they needed 60% capacity every day to breakeven. They were operating well below that, closer to 40%.

I met with the CEO of the subsidiary and was told that they were the Cadillac of psychiatric hospitals. Unfortunately, six other freestanding psychiatric hospitals entered the market at the same time. Evidently, a lot of other planners read the same journal articles about the need for such hospitals.

I've always thought a Cadillac was excessive and inefficient. I met with the controller of the subsidiary and told her about my concerns. She said that staffing standards had never been set for their facility. I felt immediate action was needed. I went to another hospital and asked if I could borrow one of their management engineers for a while. His job was to develop staffing standards at the new subsidiary. He completed his work in about two weeks. As a result, both fixed and variable components were cut, including the reduction of staff and closing one of their three hospital units.

During the year the state health department, which paid for certain services at the hospital, decided they would pay for a nine-day course of treatment as opposed to the twenty-two days they previously covered. I found it curious that accountants could make clinical decisions in health care. Even with the unforeseen reduction in volume, the subsidiary came in only slightly higher than the budgeted loss for the year. It was a significant accomplishment. This demonstrates how controlling fixed asset spending and its relationship to earnings is critical.

Lousy Job of Projecting

Part of the capital budgeting process was to follow up with a post-audit review, comparing several years of actual performance to what had been projected. The internal auditors then put together a report on their findings.

One day I was in the office of a vice president responsible for corporate analysis when he commented, "We do a lousy job of capital budgeting in this corporation."

"What do you mean?" I asked.

"Look at our post-audits. None of the projects ever generate the performance they promised."

This was a classic example of a shot gun killing everyone instead of a rifle targeting the problem areas. I said, "You're not being fair. Major projects coming from those with little experience have seldom hit the mark, but those that grow out of the field, based on experience, have a great track record."

I don't know if he liked my response, but I couldn't let him attack what I thought was a great record from my region.

Another Job Offer

One day the director of the Southern Region came in my office and asked if I was interested in applying to be the operations head/ CEO of one of his hospitals. I was flattered because there was an unwritten rule at Family Healthcare that "bean counters" were simply not qualified to be operations people.

I understood for quite some time that for finance people to be really good they had to focus on the area that they controlled: holding the line on expenses and spending. At the same time the marketers were charged with spending money and generating revenue. Finance specialists were considered less than creative while marketers were just the opposite.

The fact that he considered me worthy to jump this fence was a major compliment. However, the timing wasn't right. It would have had been necessary to relocate and I wasn't sure about the potential career path this might lead to. I thanked him for considering me and regretfully told him it just wasn't the right time.

A Creative Solution

As part of our monthly performance meeting we reviewed all major variances between actual financial performance and the budget. We would go through all line items, paying special attention to salary and wages, which accounted for more than 60 percent of expenses. When I was budget manager for the corporation we implemented a variance analysis system for staffing where management engineers set staffing standards for every department. Based on staffing patterns we would separate the difference between actual and budget into a volume, rate, and efficiency variance.

One area that always seemed beyond analysis was the contractual allowance. The contractual allowance was the difference between what we actually billed the patient and what the government would pay. The difference could be millions of dollars for the entire corporation and no one could ever explain why. This went on for years until one day I was thinking about our variance analysis for salaries and wages and how that tool might be applied to the contractual allowance figure. I was thinking way outside the box.

I looked at the assumptions that went into building the contractual allowance budget and then compared it with what actually occurred. When we built the budget we assumed the government would pay a certain rate at an average acuity level. In reality the actual rate and our acuity level ended up being quite different. I put together an analysis and went to the next monthly accountability meeting.

The vice president of finance happened to be out of town that month and so my former boss, Stanley, director of budgeting and government compliance, was sitting in for him. When we got to the variance in contractual allowance I began to explain why. I said that of the $500K variance, $100K related to volume, $250K related to a change in rate, and $150K related to acuity.

I could see that I caught Stanley off guard. The rest of the meeting was pretty bland because he was musing over what I had just explained. Later that day I received a call from Kitty, an analyst from Stanley's department, who wanted to know what I had done. I explained my methodology and showed her my simple calculations. She went back to her office and crafted a nine page report for each subsidiary to fill out every month, based on my methodology. They were going to take credit for what I had initiated and it was complete overkill. I almost regretted showing them a better way.

Property Taxes

Family Healthcare enjoyed non-profit status and therefore did not pay property taxes. It had sizable subsidiaries in several smaller communities. Governmental officials in various towns and cities, searching for additional revenue, looked longingly at this potential source of lost property taxes. One of the communities decided to send a property tax notice to a local healthcare operation to see what would happen. This set the wheels turning in several other communities that decided to follow suit. Suddenly, the corporate office was scrambling to address this new assault.

Summit meetings were called, boards of directors for each hospital were marshaled, strategies were initiated, and an almost wartime environment followed. Powerful people in high places were enlisted to defend Family Healthcare. The sequence of events that evolved was a pure demonstration of the importance of influence. As a result of pulling out all the stops, the issue was defeated, but not before it went to the state Supreme Court and back to the state taxing authority that had been sufficiently infiltrated.

The Magic Journal Entry

With the new corporate structure for vertical integration there was a mad scramble to see who could position themselves in the line of succession. One vice president, Cole, was placed in charge of a key new insurance division. A successful tenure could launch him into the position of CEO at Family Healthcare.

After two years of doing everything he could, Cole was unable to make the division profitable. A juggling of assignments put the corporate CFO, Braxton, in charge of the division. He managed it for one year. As the year was coming to a close, it appeared the same result was going to be his fate—that is until Ernest, who reported to Braxton, walked into my office one day. Ernest accused the hospitals within the Central Region of overcharging the insurance division. He said that excessive rate increases had driven hospital revenues higher than they should have been at the expense of the insurance division.

Ernest told me that a series of journal entries were going to be booked that would correct what had been overcharged. This effectively transferred profit from the hospitals to the insurance division and instantly made it profitable. These entries made it look like Braxton turned the affiliate around and was a management genius. He was now first in line of succession and Cole was out of the picture. Eventually Braxton became CEO of Family Healthcare and Cole left the company.

Centralized Functions

An analysis was done that showed each subsidiary had the same laboratory functions. The corporation decided to work toward building a central lab. However, powerful pathologists were in charge of the labs, which could prove to be a difficult hurdle to cross.

A national consultant was contracted to help with the transition. He advised that a quick fix was virtually impossible without a lot of stress on the organization. He proposed a much slower process. The first year he would hold a monthly meeting with the professionals from each subsidiary and discuss what was happening and obtain their feedback. This was a valuable lesson. Sometimes when dealing with powerful professionals, a slow process with lots of input is best.

Leaving Family Healthcare

Ernest demanded that I require certain things of the subsidiaries. When I indicated that the directive was given by Ernest, he would get angry. He wanted to swing his weight, but not take responsibility for it. He didn't understand budgeting and prided himself on managing working capital—particularly accounts receivable. His favorite employee was Clyde, who oversaw the Central Collection Agency.

One of my controllers privately complained to me that she felt the relationship with Clyde and his brother, the attorney who worked for the collection agency, was a problem. She had been an internal auditor and I took her complaint seriously, but Ernest wouldn't hear of it. He loved Clyde.

I attended a Christmas party hosted by Clyde's collection group at a local country club. The high point was Clyde giving a Christmas present to Ernest. I never felt that ingratiating oneself to a superior was required if you were a competent employee. It was obvious that Clyde was doing his best to find favor with Ernest. It made me suspicious of the relationship.

Several things Ernest did appeared to be less than professional. He always tried to elevate himself by putting people down. I guess Ernest could sense my lack of respect for him and though I was always professional, my hospitals always on budget and performing well, he was disturbed. He was a master of cookie jar accounting—manipulating the books to meet corporate targets.

When Ernest gained sufficient control over the company he demanded that all financial officers have a solid reporting line to him and a dotted line report to their operational head. I knew this would be intolerable and decided to leave Family Healthcare.

After ten years, I left Family Healthcare in January 1989. The following summer I heard about Clyde. Evidently the internal auditors discovered a problem with his operations and decided to review transactions from the previous six months. They discovered that he had been embezzling funds and stolen more than $500K in six months. Ernest immediately went to Clyde's office, locked the door, terminated Clyde on the spot, and tried to do damage control. Clyde worked for the company almost ten years, so I figure he must have taken at least several million dollars. Although Family Healthcare didn't press charges, the bonding company did. Clyde ultimately served a prison term.

Several years later when the Sarbanes-Oxley Act was passed, which required corporations to improve their accounting and financial controls, it wasn't long before Ernest was asked to leave Family Healthcare.

Monopoly or Not

Another interesting challenge that confronted Family Healthcare was their monopolistic domination of health care services in the markets where they were located. This happened to fall within my region. It became such an issue that the federal government got involved. I attended several meetings where agreements had been made to limit competition just as the government suspected.

Before the government could subpoena the information required to prove their case, Family Healthcare went through an extensive sterilization process and shredded all documents pertaining to the allegations. As attorneys became involved, the case plodded on and on. Eventually the federal government was convinced to turn over the prosecution to the state's attorney general. That year happened to be an election year. Shortly after the new attorney general was sworn in the matter was dropped.

I was curious to see if the new attorney general had been influenced by campaign contributions from Family Healthcare. I went to the secretary of state's office and requested a list of contributions made the attorney general's campaign. There was no evidence of Family Healthcare making any sizable donation. As I looked further I discovered one particular day where a long list of individuals contributed $750 each. I recognized the names of directors from various boards at FHC hospitals.

Next Position

Before I accepted my next job I began looking throughout the country for a comparable corporate finance position. I sat down to look at a map of the United States and decided I would work anywhere in the country except for North Dakota and downtown Los Angeles. I'm not sure why I made that decision before my search began, but that is how it was.

I received a call from a corporation that wanted me to fly out for an interview. An officer at one of their hospitals previously worked in my region at Family Healthcare and recommended me. The corporate office was in Fargo, North Dakota. It was February and throughout the flight I couldn't help but reflect on the irony of the situation.

I think it was the coldest weather I had ever experienced. The night before the interview, I decided to walk around the town to see what was happening. I walked about a block and nearly froze to death. The next day when we drove into the corporation's parking lot I noticed electrical outlets in front of each parking stall. They said that on very rare occasions they recommend people plug their cars in so they would start at the end of the day.

My next formal interview request came from a corporation in downtown Los Angeles. I wondered what the odds were that I would pick two locations to avoid and the first interview requests I receive come from there.

I had been teaching at a local college as an adjunct for about five years before I left FHC. The college offered me a position as a permanent faculty member when I decided to change careers and accept their offer.

Key Points

- Sometimes a loss leader is necessary to complement broader strategic success.
- Immediate intervention can avert a disaster.
- Some managers prefer to use a shotgun instead of a single rifle shot to solve a problem.
- Corporate planners with little practical experience can make poor investment decisions.
- Projects that grow out of the field can be the best investments.
- Bean counters and marketing types have very different responsibilities; management must celebrate each function and balance the two.
- Creativity can mean applying an old tool to a new and different problem.
- What one person can make simple, another person can make complex.
- Corporations are always on guard and ready to protect their franchise. They will use all possible resources to defeat the enemy.
- Allocation of revenues and/or expenses from one division to another can make a manager look good or bad—depending on who controls the books.
- Cultural change takes longer with high-power employees.
- You can't work for someone you don't respect.

- Friendship with a subordinate can create a blind spot causing the corporation to be vulnerable.
- Political rules and laws can be circumvented by creative corporate officers who want to protect their franchise.

College

I began teaching at a small private college in the fall of 1989. This afforded me time to devote to consulting work and study to support my teaching. I've found that textbooks are about ten years behind the real world. It takes time for the academic community to validate current practice. Let me give you a case in point:

Around 1990 I read an article in *Fortune* magazine about a new tool many of the Standard &Poor's (S&P) 500 companies were exploring. Economic Value Added (EVA) is almost the same concept that managerial accounting textbooks referred to as "residual income"—with a few twists. I began incorporating EVA into my courses and soon became known as the EVA professor.

Since that time I've used a valuation text by McKinsey that utilizes almost the same concept, but calls it "economic profit." The principle is very powerful. It takes the return on investment (ROI) from the DuPont model one step further. It is not about just how big the return on your investment is, but whether your return covers all your costs and generates anything in excess. By all costs, I'm referring to operating, investing, and financing. Historically, financing costs were not treated in their entirety; the cost of equity was ignored.

This new model incorporating EVA, or residual income, was a wonderful improvement on the age-old ROI.

Consulting Work

While teaching I served as a consultant with various clients. I signed a contract to consult with a state agency that regulated a service provided by private companies. We began by trying to determine an appropriate measure of how to evaluate the profitability of a company and if a rate increase was required.

My contact at the state asked for my recommendation, which I gave. He responded by suggesting ROI. I proposed another measure and he responded with ROI. After he countered my third offer with ROI, I said, "Why don't we use ROI?" He was in total agreement. Sometimes people want their own inclination validated.

One of the major companies the state regulated submitted a request for a significant rate increase. My contact at the state wanted me to review the request to see if it was appropriate. I evaluated the document and acquired a copy of the company's financial statements. I also acquired a copy of the company's payroll. I needed to have a base for comparison to determine if the salaries were within guidelines, but was having a difficult time finding comparable data for the industry. The state didn't offer much help. I found there an industry association that published a monthly magazine. When I called the magazine they would not send me copies, but did tell me they generated an annual survey of senior management compensation that was published in their December issue each year.

I investigated every source I could think of and could not obtain a copy of the magazine. Finally, on a hunch, I went to the medical library of a large local hospital. Everything I needed was on the shelf. As I compared the company salaries with national averages, the company appeared to be on the high side. As I further studied the company payroll, I noticed that several members of the president's family worked for the company and were paid quite well. I also noticed that the president's wife was listed and made an equal amount to that of the president.

On my next visit to the company I asked what functional responsibilities the president's wife had. I was told she was the CFO. That seemed curious since I had never met her. I drove by the president's home and found that it was more expensive than I would imagine his salary would command.

At a hearing the company brought in four accountants from their CPA firm, the company president, and vice president. On the other side of the table were myself and my contact at the state. The two junior accountants from the CPA firm were relatively green and could not answer the more sophisticated questions I posed. The two partners from the firm were too far removed from the detail to address the issues.

When I raised questions about compensation and the president's wife the president became angry, withdrew his application for rate increase, and demanded that all financial information be deemed confidential and proprietary.

The Russians

Throughout the years I worked for my brother at his CPA firm on special projects. I never did taxes or auditing, but occasionally I would do a simple valuation. I'll never forget the Russians.

One day my brother called and said he needed me to help two Russians determine the value of a company they wanted to buy. When we first met I was surprised to see two very serious, big-boned fellows.

The sole proprietor who operated the business quoted a $200K purchase price. One of the Russians was anxious to make the purchase, but the other was wary. It was a inventory-intensive company and I told them I knew nothing about how to value this kind of specialized inventory. Additionally, the property the business sat on was going to be a challenge.

The Russians told me they were comfortable placing a value on the land and inventory, but wanted me to look at the operations. I set up a meeting with the owner who allowed me to inspect the books and observe how the business functioned.

I discovered that he had no employees, but instead rented staff from an independent agency. His personal take-home pay for a year was not sufficient for the time he put in, let alone any return on investment. His wife did taxes on the side to cover their cost of living.

Based on his cash flow I valued the operations at just over $50,000, well below the asking price of $200K. Of course this didn't allow for the value of inventory or other assets. When the brothers received my report, they went back to the owner to renegotiate.

That was the end of our engagement, except for the bill. I submitted my invoice for the work I did and wondered what would happen next. I thought my charge was fair and may have saved them a ton of money, but I was completely intimidated by the two husky men.

My brother and I thought it best to write off the bill and chalk it up to experience, but we eventually received the payment and I was pleased.

Buying a Business

My brother called and said he had another client that was looking to purchase a business through a business brokerage. He asked if I could come along and I agreed.

We met at the seller's home, which was very impressive. He had clearly done well financially. The seller and a young business broker greeted my brother, the client, and I. "Well, if we are going to look at this business, we first need a set of financial statements," I said. The broker pulled out some papers and handed them to me.

"Is this all you have?" I asked.

"If you are any kind of businessman, that should be quite sufficient," he declared.

I looked at the limited set of numbers and soon realized there were no assets other than a large accounts receivable that was offset by an equally large accounts payable. Alarms went off in my head. If you cancelled one out with the other there were virtually no assets at all. I then asked for an income statement and cash flow statement. I received a limited set of numbers that made little sense.

The client was extremely anxious to buy the business. He was going to mortgage his home; use all his equity; and give it to this guy who basically owned no assets, not even a franchise. He was not even willing to provide a basic financial history.

The broker became defensive and tried to intimidate us, but I ignored him and opted to work with the seller. Rather than challenge him, I began asking him about his great acumen as a businessman. He could not resist talking about his accomplishments. The more he talked the more it became apparent that the business was based on utilizing marketing practices to find new customers rather than delivering a service to any fundamental, established customer base.

My brother's client was giving this guy all the equity in his home for the right to lease some equipment and space, and then find new customers for himself. When I advised against moving forward with the purchase, our client was not happy.

Great Little Company

My brother asked me to perform a valuation for one of his clients, so I began gathering the required financial information. It was a great company that performed a specialized service for a national market. Its growth over the last several years had been consistent and it was easy to project what their future would be. It had a good net income stream and was conservative in almost all aspects of its operations. I came up with a value of approximately $10 million.

Afterwards I received a call from a New York-based analyst who wanted to validate my assumptions. We exchanged notes and he was particularly interested in knowing what factors I considered in determining the WACC. I told him and he seemed satisfied. The client he represented offered to purchase this great little company for about $12 million. I felt that this was such a wonderful company with a terrific niche market that they had significant potential. The offer of $12 million was rejected.

Years later the business owners' son was in one of my MBA classes and I got to know him well. About five years after my original valuation the owners asked that I perform another valuation so they could gift stock to their son since he was about to take over the company. This time the valuation went much differently. After the last valuation the company decided to expand and built a larger facility to accommodate their projected growth.

They were growing their revenue at about 20% per year, but their expansion had created a much more erratic financial picture. They reported a couple of years of negative bottom-line. It was difficult to trend their future, but their officers assured me that they expected at least 20% revenue growth for the next several years. Because of their increased volatility of earnings, the valuation was not as high as I would have expected, but they were satisfied in using it for gifting purposes.

Through the years I have seen this company stand out among businesses in the community. I was proud to associate with them.

Selling the Business

In the fall of 1999 my brother discovered he had pancreatic cancer and decided to sell his CPA firm. I assisted him with the transaction. We tried to locate interested buyers and had several visit the office.

I'll never forget the discussion I had with one potential buyer. They seemed professional and eager to determine the value of the firm. I said, "It will be easy to determine the value of the firm, but the more important issue is integrity." I knew my brother had an incredible amount of integrity and was a hard worker. I indicated that the most critical factor was integrity; whoever bought the firm had to demonstrate the same level of integrity that my brother's clients had come to expect.

This seemed to turn them on their heels, but we were serious about not only the quality of the firm and its client list, but the quality of the individuals that would serve those clients. I think my brother was pleased that his reputation was validated. Ultimately the business was sold to a group that was able to continue the fine service my brother provided and ensure a smooth transition.

By brother's goal was to work until the end of tax season the following year. He almost made it and showed incredible courage to go to work, even when his body was racked with pain and he could hardly stand to get out of bed.

Small Nonprofit

I was asked to sit on the board of a small, local not-for-profit company. It was a great experience, but I think I was disruptive from time to time. At year-end the auditors came to the board meeting ready to present year-end financials. The income statement reflected a modest positive net income. I quickly turned to the cash flow statement and saw that the cash flow from operations was negative.

I asked why the company was not able to translate a positive net income into cash flow. Everyone in the room was surprised and didn't quite know how to react. Looking at the detail, the reason was a buildup of accounts receivable. I didn't want to make a bigger issue of the matter so I let it slide.

The next year when the auditors brought the year-end statements to the board, they watched me carefully as I checked the positive net income against the cash flow statement. It reflected a positive cash flow. Their faces were smug with satisfaction until I looked at the detail and saw that an excessive buildup of accounts payable was the reason.

I asked what was going on with accounts payable. They sheepishly replied the company had stopped paying them in November. It was obvious they were concerned about my impending cash flow question, and by stopping the payment to vendors, the excessive cash that was built-up would put them in the black. I suppose they didn't think I would look at the details. It was an embarrassing moment for the company.

The next year I pressed the company to present a strategic plan to the board and they responded with a wonderful assessment of the market and their position in it. I inquired about their long-term growth goal. As a nonprofit they had no access to investors and a constant buildup of accounts receivable put them in a cash crunch. Consequently, obtaining a line of credit from a local bank was a continual problem. They needed to understand that a stronger bottom-line would generate the funds needed to grow and take some pressure off short-term borrowing. It was almost impossible to convince them that they needed a strong bottom-line. Their culture dictated that a not-for-profit was literally meant there was no net profit.

My reasoning for creating a stronger bottom-line was because each year their expenses were increasing with the rate of inflation—approximately 3%. If the market was growing at a 3% population growth, their revenues would need to grow annually at about 6% to maintain market share and cover increased expenses. As revenues increased, so would assets like accounts receivable, inventory, and work cash. A buildup of these assets had to be financed through short-term borrowing, or the more preferred method, retaining net income. It was difficult for them to grasp the concept.

A couple of years later the company enjoyed a strong year and the bottom line was better than usual. We changed audit firms from a relatively small company to a larger one. When the new auditors presented the year-end statements, I was shocked at their recommendation.

The president reported that the market did not look good for the coming year. Therefore, the auditors suggested an increase in allowance for doubtful accounts with an offsetting increase in bad debt expense for the year. This cookie jar technique would reserve some of this year's bottom line in case it was needed in the future. I couldn't believe what I was hearing. This was post Sarbanes-Oxley, Enron, and all the other shenanigans, and the auditors were still playing games. Wow.

I transitioned off the board but felt I made some significant contributions. I was the one that pushed them to begin a foundation to raise more money. I pushed them to examine their lease agreement for the building they were in. Subsequently, they moved to a new building. Hopefully I provided more insight into earnings, growth, and integrity in accounting.

ESOP Once More

Guest lecturers from major corporations around the country visited the college from time to time. On one occasion the financial officer for an international company gave a speech to a crowded auditorium. He was brilliant and reaffirmed what I knew to be true.

Their company was reported to be extremely progressive with its management style. It had almost no hierarchy and all the employees fully participated in ownership of the company. It sounded like a real democratic company. Everyone was happy and maximizing their potential.

After the lecture a few faculty members took the guest speaker out to dinner. Sitting directly across from the financial officer, I had the opportunity to learn more about the democratic ownership of the company. I asked him about how it worked and he said, "Well, we have an employee stock ownership plan."

I'm sure I was the only person at the table who knew what he was talking about. Employees participated in the plan to gain an economic interest in the company by purchasing company stock. But there was no democratic voice offered to management in such an arrangement. I asked what percent of the total company stock was owned by the ESOP. He said with pride that it was 15%. The family still controlled 85% of the company.

Broker's Commissions

One of my students was working in the insurance industry and prepared an analysis of brokers' commissions. He reported that brokers routinely made 20% of the insurance company's total charge. I wondered what the college was paying and began to investigate.

The college's insurance broker was on the board of trustees. When I asked the college's chief financial officer (CFO) what the broker made on our account, he didn't know. Later I found out the broker employed an agent with a golf handicap of 5 to handle our account. He must have spent a lot of time on the golf course.

I let the matter go and didn't do anything more about it until the college changed presidents. The new CEO wanted to change the board from a group of takers to a group of givers. She launched a task force to look at our insurance and I asked if I could serve on it. A request for proposals (RFP) was sent to the major insurance brokers in the area resulting in numerous candidates. .

The proposals were all interesting. When it came to the question of how much the broker would make, the answers ranged from a percentage of the account to a fixed fee. The last presenter was our current broker. When he came into the meeting it was obvious he was disgusted.

He made his pitch and told us it was none of our business how much he made on the account. His services were terminated.

The new broker's charge was transparent. It just so happened that the charge did not go down. What did happen was the service skyrocketed. We found places of overlapping coverage and other inefficiencies that were cleaned up.

At the Airport

My wife and I were picking up our bags at the airport when we returned from a wonderful vacation. As we waited, I heard someone calling my name. As I turned I saw a former student approaching me. I've had a great number of students through the years and I can usually remember their faces, but have a more difficult time remembering their names. I've worked out a system with my wife where she initiates an introduction by saying: "Hello, I'm Christine." The former student usually responds by introducing himself to her and stating his name. Problem solved.

I didn't need her this time. His name came to me instantly. "Hello Leon, how are you?"

After some small talk he said, "I want to thank you for getting me my job." I didn't recall writing him a letter of recommendation or even getting a reference call.

He said, "I was in the final round of job interviews and each of the finalists were asked to define WACC and EVA. I was the only one who knew the answers and was given the job. Thanks for preparing me."

Key Points

- Sometimes a client wants a consultant to validate their own inclination.
- You can't value what you don't understand.
- A seller may think his business is wonderful, but if there is no dependable stream of cash flow, there is no value.
- The true value of any business is the integrity of the owners.
- Every once in a while you find a great little company that is a privilege to associate with.
- Most small companies are always in need of cash.
- Sometimes business people who serve on boards of directors don't look closely at the financial statements.
- Accountants pride themselves on being able to manipulate the numbers.
- Some people work with illusions instead of facts.

What FIRE Represents

What have I learned about basic business practices throughout the past forty-something years? It has become apparent that for any business to survive it needs a strong set of financial controls. It is difficult for students to grasp the various aspects that are involved and most MBA students don't want to know the details. For them leadership is what is important. I can't fault them—a competitive advantage in any business is critical.

I've learned there are two general types of people in business: marketers who look to generate revenue, and number-crunchers who control expenses. Both types are absolutely essential to the health of any business. I've never considered myself to be a marketer, so I can only speak to the financial side of the business.

As I teach MBA classes I am continually confronted with both marketing and financial experts. Through the years, I've tried to help marketers understand enough about finance to have a basic working-knowledge of the industry. This book is full of financial control ideas, but I don't expect a non-finance person to fully appreciate all of them. As a result I've simplified the most important areas into an acronym I call FIRE. By controlling the areas represented by this acronym, any person can hopefully get by.

Fixed Assets

The first letter, *F*, stands for fixed assets. Every business needs to realize that expenditures for fixed assets are necessary. The 1920s case of General Motors demonstrates with significant evidence what most companies continue to forget. Entities need to remember that a careful review process ensures that buying tangible assets will contribute to the profitability of the company.

In my own experience I've reviewed hundreds and hundreds of capital budgeting proposals for the acquisition of fixed assets. Since I began my career in finance I have seen more proposals than I care to mention. Textbooks continue to focus on creating capital budgeting proposals because it is critical to financial control.

Every business manager should try to project where the business is going and consider the possibilities. This takes discipline and a system of review and analysis.

Inventory

The second letter, *I*, stands for inventory. I produced inventory at the bakery, stored and sold inventory at the department store, and clipped coupons from an inventory of negotiable bonds at the trust department. Even at the CPA firm it was necessary to confirm the inventory count to verify it actually existed.

In 1920 General Motors almost went out of business because of a lack of inventory management and controls. In the book *My Years With General Motors*, by Alfred P. Sloan, (which writer, professor, and management consultant Peter Drucker called the best book on management ever written) the chapter about financial controls addresses the rigorous process the company went through to gain control of their inventory.

Working at Family Healthcare I saw how loose inventory controls over supplies was a standard problem and a source of increased expenses. Business students must understand the importance of tight inventory controls.

Receivables

The third letter, *R*, stands for receivables. . No other area is as important. If you don't collect the money from the sale, you are simply giving your product or service away. At Emerson Advertising the control of working capital pivoted on the extension of credit and managing receivables. All cash management tools supported the constant need for liquidity and collecting receivables.

At Family Healthcare cash was critical. We had one person whose entire job was cash management, but it took hundreds of people throughout the subsidiaries and Central Collection Agency to manage billing and follow up. At one time a portion of our receivables from a government contract became a problem. They were being paid within a relatively decent time frame. For some reason the state decided that prisoners at the state penitentiary could process the invoices. Our receivables for that contract went from thirty to more than 100 days. It was a mess. The corporate office wanted to delay the payment of payables from ten to twenty days to offset some of the cash exposure, but the board opposed saying the image of the corporation would be damaged. They were willing to take the hit for the sake of reputation.

Many companies have gone out of business because they haven't paid enough attention to cash management and the collection of receivables. The best thing Jonas did at Emerson Advertising was to charge the sales executives with collecting receivables from the clients they served.

Excess Earnings

The last letter, *E*, stands for excess earnings. General Motors developed ROI and DuPont executives perfected it in the 1920s. It has been called the DuPont model in almost every finance and accounting textbook ever since. It is a great centralized tool for managing in a decentralized company. The concept of excess earnings that I refer to can go by several names: Stern Stewart & Consulting Co. branded it as EVA, McKinsey & Company calls it economic profit, and managerial textbooks have called it residual income for the longest time.

The concepts are similar and take ROI to the next level. It integrates the tools used in asset management, net income management, and cost of capital. It is a wonderful tool and the ultimate metric for managing the company. The tool operates on the theory that the company needs to generate enough revenue to cover all operating expenses, financing costs, and related taxes. The Achilles' heel for most managers is the cost of equity within financing costs. If a company has nothing remaining after deducting these expenses and costs from revenue, then it is breaking even. But if it can generate excess earnings, then it is adding value to the company.

By utilizing the financial controls represented by FIRE, any business executive will help ensure their company is safe and sound.

Postscript

Opportunity

Many MBA students want to get an advanced degree so they can advance their career. I try to explain that they are missing a wonderful opportunity. They need to become intrapreneurs and take advantage of the possibilities where they are.

The first step is to find a mentor at the company who holds a senior position. That mentor would preferably be the president of the company. If the president truly takes them under their wing, the potential of success is greatly enhanced. The second step is to learn to like the person you want to emulate, sincerely respect what they have accomplished and their abilities, and let them know you want to learn from them.

If you are taken under their wing, it will make the process of growth and development much easier. The next step is to learn as much as possible about the company, its products, and market so you can see the possibilities. Next, you need to think outside the box and look for ways to marry new technologies, concepts, and ideas with existing processes and products. Sometimes it is as simple as using an old method in a new way. Never be afraid to rely on your own passions and strengths.

Every company goes through a capital budgeting process where employees offer new ideas that require an up-front outlay of significant funds for machinery, equipment, software, or marketing blitz. I say, "Suppose you were to go to the CEO and ask for a million dollars to acquire a new machine. Would they laugh? It all depends on how you present your argument."

If the company is making a 12% return on their investment and it costs 10% to secure financing, then they are effectively generating a 2% excess earnings. Suppose an employee came up with an idea that complemented the company's core business and could generate a 20% return on its investment. Wouldn't the CEO be interested? I tell my MBA students that it is not only getting a job, but getting an idea. The last thing to do is package the idea appropriately, enthusiastically sell the idea, and protect it so someone else doesn't get the credit and promotion.

THE
MERCHANT

By

Gaylen K. Bunker

Preface

It is apparent that many students with graduate business degrees are ill prepared for the responsibilities being thrust upon them. Hired into management positions and destined for a rapid rise to the executive suite, these business professionals apply academically acquired analytical techniques to real-world problems with mixed success. They lack practical knowledge of business and how it functions. One astute observer suggested what these "young stars" need is a course in old-fashioned business: how to be merchants.

The Merchant of Damascus

Long ago Constantinople, Turkey, was the center of world trade and the crossroads of goods from the east and west. Merchants from around the world came to its markets to see wonderful and exotic products from India, China, Egypt, Scandinavia, Russia, and the West.

Matthew, a young man from modest circumstances, went to a prominent merchant of Constantinople to ask for the hand of his daughter. The merchant praised the youth for his ambition, but counseled him about how marriage is a vehicle to solidify position between wealthy families. The daughter was beautiful and cared deeply for Matthew. The merchant said he would consent to the marriage if the youth could demonstrate he had sufficient capacity.

"How is that done?" Matthew asked.

The merchant said, "Show that you understand the laws of the merchant." With that the conference was over.

Matthew sat despondently wondering what to do. Then he thought of Abu, the merchant from Damascus, Syria. Abu was reputed to be one of the most respected of all merchants. Surely he must know the laws of the merchant. Matthew went to where Abu sold his wares and watched the hustle of the marketplace. At the end of the day Matthew approached Abu and said, "You are so busy. To have an assistant would be a great blessing."

"No" Abu responded.

Matthew insisted, "I am very diligent and quick to learn."

"No," Abu repeated. Pressing the issue Matthew said, "I desire to work and learn to be a merchant as you are."

Abu finally said, "I see persistence in you. Let me give you a test. I will tell you one of the laws of the merchant. These are from the *Book of Secrets* that are told to many people, but few grasp their significance and truly understand. They seem to be common sense, but that is their disguise. If you treat them casually, they will not bless your life and you will not become a great merchant."

Matthew said, "Very well, I am ready."

Know Your Goods

Abu said, "You must know your goods. What do you think about that?"

Matthew looked around at the wares that were spread before Abu and stuttered, "I suppose a merchant needs to know what he is selling."

"Is that it?" Abu said.

Matthew looked a little forlorn and helpless. Abu picked up a beautiful earthenware jar and placed it in Matthew's hands. "Tell me about this!"

"It is a jar. Quite heavy, smooth, and beautifully colored in purple rings. It is as tall as a man's foot and its opening larger than an outstretched hand," Matthew responded.

Abu said, "You have given me a physical description, but does that mean you know it?"

Matthew seemed lost and did not know what to say. "Do you know where it was made and by who? Do you know what materials went into its manufacture? Do you know why it is designed the way it is? Do you know what the materials and construction will tolerate? Do you know what the purple rings signify?" Abu whispered with pointed directness at Matthew. Matthew responded that he did not know to every question.

Abu continued, "Do you know how it came to be here and which caravan brought it? Do you know if the merchants in that caravan could be trusted? Were they representing themselves or the people who made it? Were they desperate or not? Do you know if the climatic change from where the piece originated to its current location compromised its integrity and usefulness? Do you know if there are a great many of these jars or if this is one of a kind? Do you know how many of these are on display in this marketplace? Do you know what other merchants are saying about this jar? Do you know how many people have purchased a jar such as this in the past? Do you know how this jar can be put to use, what it is best suited for, and what can safely be stored in it?"

The questions were coming fast and furious from Abu as his voice became louder. Matthew could only stand there holding the jar, looking down at it and shaking his head from side to side. "What do you say now?" Abu asked.

Matthew raised his head, looked at Abu and with determination said, "I can learn." Abu shot back, "You can learn what?" Matthew hesitated for a moment with his mind racing and said, "I can learn all of that about this jar."

Abu raised his open hand up in front of his face as if to physically challenge Matthew. "And I can learn much more. I can learn about each of the items you sell…" Abu tilted his head to the side with his brow furrowed. "And I can... learn the principle. I must know my goods," Matthew concluded.

Abu dropped his hand, straightened up, and said to Matthew, "And how will you do this?"

Matthew answered, "You will teach me, and I will dedicate myself to doing and learning everything you say. I will be your slave and your servant."

Abu finally agreed:

> Very well, you may be my servant, but you will not begin here in the marketplace. You must spend the next several weeks travelling to where many of our products are made. You must watch carefully and learn what makes a superior and inferior good. There are many who are lazy and will cheat you, if they can. You must be sharp of mind and carefully inspect all that passes before you. You must know the standard of each ware and the fraudulent and counterfeit practices that accompany them.
>
> You must know which items are subject to spoilage, how to package and preserve them, and how to fold and display them.

Just as you have made me your mentor, you must develop many mentors who will train you and share their secrets.

The world is a balance between consumption and investment. Wise men minimize consumption and maximize investment. If they perceive that you are a worthy vessel for their knowledge, then they will invest that knowledge in you. If you receive their counsel lightly and do not take it to heart, they will no longer waste their time on your behalf. Listen carefully and take notes.

Matthew was diligent in all he did. He was the first to arrive in the morning and the last to leave at night. When the other young men would frolic in the evenings, he would take notes and compare what he learned that day with what he learned before. His knowledge grew as he became a constant fixture at the manufacture and the marketplace. He became acquainted with many people and they came to know him well. He learned by walking around, observing, and talking to people.

At the conclusion of his travels he went to the girl's father and reported that he would be in possession of the laws of the merchant, but it would take a little time. The father was impressed that Matthew had Abu as his mentor. He said, "I will wait before giving my daughter's hand in marriage." As Matthew returned to Abu he noticed the caravan of the Radhanites, Jewish traveling merchants, entering the city. He asked Abu about them.

Pursue Information

Abu said, "Question, evaluate, and trade the irrelevant. What do you think about that?"

"Information is important," Matthew said.

"It is critical," emphasized Abu.

The merchant then recalled the words of Sun Tzu:

The great Chinese warlord, Sun Tzu, said that foreknowledge is what elevates the enlightened prince and wise general allowing them to conquer the enemy and achieve unsurpassed results. Sun Tzu said this foreknowledge does not come from spirits, Gods, calculations, or analysis of past events, but from men who know the situation. You must be delicate and subtle to gain the truth. You must judge men to know if they are sincere, truthful, and truly intelligent.

You must identify what motivates them. What is their nature? What kind of habits do they have? What is their ultimate goal? What are their fears and weaknesses? Who pays them and dictates their time? You must know if your customers are poor and seek basic goods, or rich and desire ornaments. Does their culture drive them to buy one thing and forbid another?

You must be careful of those who might lead you astray with false reports. You must inquire of matters in minute detail. Those who are your eyes and ears and provide you with the purest information must be rewarded generously.

Timing is important. You must realize there is a trade-off between what is relevant and what is reliable. A caravan of Varangians once came from Scandinavia to sell a large amount of furs and swords. Because I had carefully inquired of the Radhanites about conditions in Scandinavia, I learned a lot of things in advance. I knew if quantities were great or small, if prices were cheap or dear, if sales were good or poor, and if the routes were safe or free. I had to be one of the first to know in order to avoid loss.

Early information was necessary to make decision, but there was some question about its reliability. If I took the time to confirm the information as being reliable, then it would no longer be relevant. Question carefully from multiple sources and determine who you can trust.

Abu taught Matthew that the marketplace is full of information and it comes from a variety of sources. Sometime information is exchanged between sources. One must sift through the data to determine what is critical and relevant to the business he is in. The information must be

111

verified before others learn of it. Keep the information that is relevant to your enterprise confidential and trade the useless information with others.

Matthew watched as Abu worked the marketplace garnering knowledge from the caravans as they entered the city. Abu then bid Matthew to do likewise. Matthew was eager, but clumsy as he continued to learn through trial and error. However, Abu was pleased with the progress Matthew was making.

Detail and Global

One day Abu said, "Precisely record, synthesize, and generalize. What do you think about that?"

Matthew said, "I have watched you for many days and you are meticulous at keeping records. You never overlook anything and you write everything down."

Abu explained the importance of maintaining records:

I do that so I know where I am and what value to place on things. Value is important to the success of a merchant. If you price items too low or too high you will fail. Records of past dealings provide a basis for comparison and show trends, but they must always be kept in perspective. Some merchants never learn that detailed records

112

allow them the freedom to see the big picture.

The records and numbers are not the business, but a picture of the business. The numbers measure the health of the business and communicate information about the enterprise. The numbers don't tell you what is happening, but they do signal when to ask questions.

The only critical error in any business is to run out of cash. If you run out of cash then you are through. The merchant who runs out of cash did not pay attention to the numbers and records.

Sometimes it is tedium and drudgery to evaluate the numbers, but it is this effort that gives a merchant freedom. Some never see the big picture and are tied to their records. Some never understand the details and are lost in the big picture.

Along with records you must have a vision of the future. Having perspective and knowing the market's potential is the basis for setting value. You must have records of the past. You must calculate costs and profits quickly. You must understand market potential. You must set value correctly.

"Value?" Matthew questioned. "It seems to change with each new ruler and trend."

Abu further explained the premise of record keeping:

To know value you must understand the context within which you are working. Regarding rulers, I have seen many come and go in different cities. Let me just say that equality and liberty cannot coexist. Let me tell you the story of Solon.

He was born to a wealthy Phoenician family living on the isle of Cypress. His father lost the family's wealth helping others. Perhaps this was intentional; Solon was a slovenly youth who enjoyed being wealthy.

With no means of support Solon worked for many years and travelled the world learning the laws of the merchant. He became wealthy and highly respected. When he finally decided to settle in Athens, he found a city on the verge of a revolution. The wealthy had amassed such great fortunes they were able to charge outrageous terms for debt and were driving most of the poor into financial slavery. War was about to ensue when a few wise merchants were able to get Solon elected as head of the government.

He became known as the "great law giver" because he passed laws that stabilized things and avert war. He passed a law that all debts were to be forgiven. This was a radical step which the wealthy hated, but it worked.

Solon told a friend that the law was there to help mankind. His friend challenged the idea and said the law was like a spider's web that traps the poor and allows the wealthy to break through.

Ideologically government should exist to establish free markets, but in reality the powerful and egocentric manipulate governments to ensure certain monopolies and oligopolies are protected. We seldom have pure economics, but often we have "egonomics."

Governments seem to move in cycles. If there is freedom, the brightest and best will collect wealth to the detriment of the poor. People then give up freedom to ensure equality from a benevolent dictator, which inevitably leads from a good ruler to a bad ruler with heavy-handed controls. The people then seek freedom which takes us back to the beginning.

Trade and the merchant will exist irrespective of the type of government. If freedom exists then most people work within the system, but if special privilege is protected, then people feel justified in trading in covert or black markets. Nevertheless, you must keep records to know where you are.

Matthew's next assignment was to review past records, learn how to log entries in the books, and quickly calculate sums and ratios in his head.

Select Good Agents

In time Abu said, "Select and hire the best to represent you. What do you think about that?"

"In business there are people you must trust to act as agents because a person can't do everything himself. The best agents are those who are successful," Matthew said.

"That is correct," Abu said. "A merchant must trust others to do those things that he cannot. Above all, an agent must be trustworthy and reliable. This is usually someone who is well-off and has devoted himself to his business and is highly experienced. The price of his service may be more than others of lesser commitment and standing, but he is well worth it."

"I think integrity is a variable thing," Matthew noted.

Abu agreed, "That is true. Even people who are the most honest can be driven to hedge the truth. Taxes are a perfect example. When taxes are low there is a high degree of compliance, but when taxes increase to a certain point, even the most virtuous people will look for ways to avoid paying. They almost feel it is an obligation or right."

"Can anyone be trusted?" Matthew asked.

Abu offered these thoughts:

You have to watch even the best agents and always do a cost-benefit analysis. It is sometimes difficult to assess the cost and benefits. You cannot always quantify all the costs or all the benefits.

Some people feel that if the benefits exceed the costs then everything is acceptable. I think it should be more like the golden ratio of 1.618 that the ancient Greeks used. This ratio appears in nature with a great degree of regularity. I often have used it as a guide in measuring benefits to costs.

"Are you saying that benefits should be 1.618 times the costs?" Matthew inquired.

"Yes, that is an excellent relationship," confirmed Abu.

Matthew listened carefully and in this regard showed that he was focused and indeed had capacity. At the marketplace Abu required Matthew to select a caravan with which to entrust a shipment of goods bound for Venice. After some examination he cast his lot with the Radhanites. Abu asked why Matthew made that choice.

"These Jews are experienced, have a strong guard, and are great in number. It is rumored that they travel from China to Spain and from Egypt to the far north," Matthew said.

"Their price to carry is higher than that of the band of Russes," complained Abu.

"We should pay the price because it reduces the risk of loss. I think you have been trying to teach me that sometimes paying the lowest price results in loss, while paying a fair price for quality results in benefits far in excess, even to the golden ratio," countered Matthew.

"Well said," responded Abu.

Those Compelled

Abu then said, "Those who are compelled are easiest to deal with. What do you think about that?"

"I suppose it is easier to buy low and sell high when you deal with people who are motivated," Matthew said.

Remembering his early career, Abu said, "When I started out I tried to sell goods to people who had no need for them. It was the most miserable experience. I had products to sell and was constantly searching for a good market. Then I discovered the secret was finding a market that was in need of products. I now feel I'm better serving the people when I give them what they want. Likewise, when I take from those who are anxious to sell, I am serving them."

"I find it interesting that you speak of service when you are making a nice profit," Matthew cynically observed.

Abu clarified the significance of good service:

Let me tell you a story. Hiram, the great Phoenician king of Tyre, contracted with

Solomon to build him a temple in Jerusalem. This was about 1000 BC and Hiram sensed Solomon's great need. The service provided by Hiram benefited them both.

Some merchants sell a few items with a high markup. I have never been one of those, but instead tried to sell in great volume. I learned that if I could cut the price and sell significantly more items, my margin would be lower, but my overall profits would be higher. The greater profit allowed me to expand my business and sell even more items. When I lowered my prices I was allowing more customers the opportunity to purchase something they could not afford otherwise. I was providing a service, I was expanding, and even more customers could be reached.

Unfortunately people are divided into three types. There are the 5% who lead out, are creative, and make things happen. There are the 25% who are responsible and carry out the direction set by the creative. Then there are the 70% who follow, which will be your typical market.

The next season was upon them and Matthew diligently applied himself to learning all that he could. Abu was impressed by Matthew's apparent grasp of the concepts they had discussed.

Abu had frequent contact with the father of the girl Matthew desired. On one such occasion the two men discussed the young man.

Abu said, "Matthew has a definite aptitude for the merchant trade. He is quick to learn from his own experience and leverages that with my instruction."

The girl's father responded, "Will he be one of the great merchants?"

"It is possible," responded Abu. "It is possible."

Greed Makes a Slave

Abu later said to Matthew, "Never surrender to the slavery of greed. What do you think about that?"

"I think this is a continuation of law five. I accused you of profiting from those who were in need," Matthew said.

"That may be true, but nevertheless, this law stands alone," Abu said. "The truly great merchant does not serve others to become rich, but becomes rich in order to serve others."

Matthew admitted, "It is a bit confusing."

Abu added, "I am a Muslim and you are a Christian. We deal with Jewish traders, but the laws of the merchant are the same for all. The great Buddha taught that he who seeks wealth should cast it away rather than let it corrupt him. He said that he who is rich and uses his wealth to benefit mankind, puts his whole heart into his enterprise, and uplifts society will be a blessing to all."

Abu continued, "Giving and getting, logic, and greed are very strong forces that fight against each other. It is said that riches and virtue struggle along life's journey together. Virtue must carry the baggage of riches, which cannot be left behind. Just as an army is hindered in its march to victory by its baggage, and thus may lose the battle, riches can prove to be too overwhelming for virtue to survive."

Abu then spoke of markets and war:

The commerce of war destroys mankind, but free markets and open commerce level and lift everyone. Free markets require logic and judgment from the merchant to succeed. When a merchant is able to restrict markets and create a monopoly for himself he becomes lazy and greedy. I do sell to those in need, but it is to assist them in satisfying their needs.

I am reminded of the slave Narcissus. When Claudius became the Roman Emperor in 41 AD he was weak. His slave, Narcissus, became powerful and dominated Claudius. Perhaps this new freedom was too much for Narcissus for he soon became a slave again, this time to greed.

At one time Narcissus was the wealthiest person in the Roman Empire. Instead of using his power to help the people, he succumbed to greed and sowed the seeds of his own destruction. It is curious how some slaves will work to become a freeman only to become slaves to greed.

"Maybe Narcissus could never adapt to freedom. Maybe he only understood slavery," Matthew replied.

Pursue Good Fortune

Abu then said, "Pursue what brings you good fortune and joy. What do you think about that?"

"I know you sell some goods but not others. Is it because of this seventh law?" Matthew asked.

Abu emphasized the importance of following your own path:

Yes. You see, as a young merchant I tried a variety of markets and goods. Some were successful, but many were not. I soon learned what I was good at and what made me happy. As you learn about the merchant trade you will inclined to emulate your mentor. You will want to do exactly as you have seen me do. That is good to an extent, but you are a different person with a unique set of talents and abilities. It may take time, but you will discover your own path. If you are successful you will learn the laws of the merchant and end up a very different person than I am. You will probably sell goods in different markets. You may even become an agent and sell services instead. That is the way it should be.

Perhaps the best story about someone who followed their own path is that of Joseph. He was sold as a slave into Egypt by his brothers when he was seventeen years old and remained in bondage until he was thirty-three.

"I'm not sure I see much good fortune there," Matthew sarcastically replied.

Abu, ignoring the comment, continued with the story:

No matter what position Joseph found himself in, he was always able to turn it to his advantage through hard work, strict obedience to his master, and a positive attitude. People revered him for his integrity and calmness in difficult times. Ultimately he followed his instincts and talents by interpreting the Pharaoh's dream and became prime minister of Egypt.

My basic philosophy is that our focus must be external, not internal. I also believe we must love what we do and not fear the future. If we love what we do and focus on others—instead of being driven by fear and selfishness, joy will be ours.

In business, the key is not what you sell or where, but that you understand the basic laws.

Matthew looked puzzled. "I am not sure that I understand this law very well."

"You can't fully understand it until you have lived it. Then it will be clear," Abu said. "It is sufficient now for you to reflect on it. Remember, patience is the key. Some scholars have spoken of faith, hope and love as the three eternal states. Let me say that faith is being patient with your God, hope is being patient with yourself, and love is being patient with others."

"It is so hard to be patient," Matthew thought aloud.

Abu countered, "It is easy. Just remember to do something else in the meantime. The more we sacrifice for something the more we love it. The more we love it the more we sacrifice for it. You have sacrificed a great deal these past months to learn the laws of the merchant and I have seen you grow in your love for them."

Gifts and Rebates

One day Abu said, "Rebates to buyers and gifts to suppliers. What do you think about that?"

"It is curious. You say that just as I was going to ask about the gift you gave that trader," Matthew noted.

"This is a teaching moment," Abu said.

"It seems you are always sweetening the exchange with some small offering. You have done that repeatedly over the last two seasons. The other party feels as though they are getting a little something extra, something they didn't pay for. It probably makes them feel good, but I've wondered if you can afford it," Matthew questioned.

Abu tried to help Matthew understand the concept:

> I can't afford not to. I am reminded of Pasion, the ancient Greek banker. He lived at the time of Socrates and went from being a slave to the wealthiest person in Athens. Timotheus, the great Athenian general, was once entertaining friends. Without adequate provision Timotheus borrowed valued items from Pasion and failed to return some of the more expensive pieces.
> Pasion said nothing, but considered the items gifts. Gifts to customers come in a lot of different forms. Pasion, the most influential financier in Athens, often financed Timotheus' battles, and in return, received tremendous profits when the spoils were brought back.
> You must make friends of your patrons and not patrons of your friends. It is a sad merchant who tries to convert every friend into a customer. This is a quick way to lose friends. On the other hand, if you go the extra mile to make your customers feel good about their transaction, they will come back every time. The key is to make sure the price is sufficient to cover the cost of the goods, the cost of gifts, taxes, and a fair

profit. This is tricky sometimes a Do you know what the greatest gift you can give is?

"Something of tangible value," Matthew answered.

"No. The greatest gift you can give is a sincere thank you. In most financial transactions I try to give something of tangible value, but when I express heartfelt thanks, I am trying to show the person that I respect them. That is the most important thing of all."

Spend Less Than You Make

At the end of the season Abu said, "Keep a portion as permanent wealth. What so you think about that?"

"I am not sure," Matthew responded.

Abu explained what he meant:

From the profits of every sale I take a portion to reinvest in the business. The remaining money goes toward personal expenses. If sales are slow I still reinvest, but have to reduce my expenses accordingly. As the merchant invests, his business grows and the merchant's capacity increases. As capacity increases, the merchant is better able to survive difficult times and reduce overall risk. I use 10% as my guide. Many merchants never learn this law and struggle from season to season.

Do you remember the story of Joseph who was sold into Egypt? He saved during the good times so there were sufficient funds in times of need. Those who had not saved were at the mercy of the Pharaoh and his storehouse.

"If a merchant can live on very little in hard times, then why not live on that amount all the time? The excess that is reinvested could grow even faster," Matthew offered.

"Balance is required in all things," Abu suggested. "Sometime you may want to invest more because of opportunity. To be constantly deprived of the good things in life can drive a person to become miserly. You must remember law six and not grow on account of greed, but grow to increase your capacity to serve."

"I've seen men work endlessly and produce very little personal wealth. They give good service to their employers and customers but seem to be miserable," Matthew said.

"It has been said that industry and frugality are the primary ways to success in business. Many people are busy and work hard, but are burdened by debt. They spend more than they make and seem unable to live within their means. So, between industry and frugality, the first is essential. The latter, however, is the key to security and peace. You must enjoy life and what you do, but you must protect your assets," Abu counseled.

Matthew replied, "It seems that the wealthy are always looking to exercise control over the poor."

"That is always the way," Abu said. "Generally the laws are made to control the masses while the wealthy find ways to circumvent the laws. It is always a challenge to work hard, but be paid fairly for your efforts. In some societies it is impossible."

Keep Within Bounds

Lastly Abu said, "Don't reach beyond your own bound. What do you think about that?"

"Do not try to be bigger than what you are," Matthew said with certainty.

Abu agreed, but clarified the point:

> In a way that is correct. Once I had an opportunity to take my own caravan from Damascus to Antioch, Turkey. It was an exciting prospect, but I was a small merchant. I would have extended myself to the point of all-or-nothing. I could not hire sufficient guards and the risks were high. It required high leverage attained by borrowing money. If I was successful I would make a fortune in a short time, but if I failed my life as a merchant would have been over. I loved what I was doing too much to take that chance. Being patient and waiting for the right opportunity is critical. After many seasons the opportunity came again. This time I was ready. I reduced the

risk to an acceptable level and was successful.

Aesop recited the fable about a lion and wild ass forming a partnership regarding hunting. The lion was so dominant that he took all the spoils. This is a warning that in business you should never form alliances or tie yourself to people who will dominate the relationship. A man should estimate his capacity and know his own power.

Sometimes slow growth from an investment with true value offers the greatest gain. Those who are after quick growth and immediate success often find disaster."

Matthew said, "You talk about leverage. What is that?"

"Leverage is the use of other people's resources. It is a necessary part of doing business, but you must be cautioned not to be excessive. There has always been a prohibition on the payment of interest, yet it is a fact of life. Some call it interest, some call it a return of their investment, and some call it a payment for expenses. Whatever name it goes by, excessive interest will be your ruin. Be prudent. Always measure risk and the related costs associated with it," concluded Abu.

Epilogue: Fulfillment

At the end of the second season Matthew returned to the father of the girl he desired. He said, "I have learned a lot these past two seasons. I have learned the ten laws of the merchant. My capacity has increased, but I have more to learn."

The father replied, "You have done well. I will grant permission for you to marry my daughter."

"Thank you for your trust, but it would be foolish to marry now. If it is acceptable to you, I would like to wait another season. There is still a lot to learn and my needs have changed. I do not desire a wife, but a companion who understands my work. I should require that you teach your daughter the ten laws of the merchant. If at the end of the next season she understands them then it will be a pleasure to accept her hand," Matthew said.

At first the father was taken aback, but he realized that Matthew's capacity had increased more than he thought. He saw wisdom in the request and agreed.

At the end of the next season the two were married. They became a great household of merchants in the city and grew to dominate much of commerce. They had learned their lessons well and blessed the lives of all they came in contact with.

The couple lived in difficult times where the conflict between ideologies and cultures stimulated wars. Matthew and his family were forced to flee and Constantinople was never the same. The family reestablished itself in the west, applied the ten laws of the merchant, and became a founding force in the great merchant trade of Europe. Matthew and his wife were careful to teach their children the ten laws, and ultimately established a dynasty.

Merchant Manager

Know Your Goods
1. Do you know everything about the history of your products and markets?
2. Have you personally visited the source of your products?
3. Do you read the literature relating to your product or service on a regular basis?
4. Do you know your market share?
5. Do you know the strategic advantage of your products or services?

Pursue Information
1. Do you belong to an association?
2. Do you communicate regularly with influential people?
3. Do you routinely talk with regulators, competitors, suppliers, and customers?
4. Do you validate or verify information provided by other sources?
5. Do you assess the value of the information?

Detail and Global
1. Do you understand you company's financial statements?
2. Do you know how financial statements are adjusted to manage earnings?
3. Do you usually participate in strategic decision making sessions?
4. Have you done a strengths, weaknesses, opportunities, and threats analysis?

5. Do you often project the value of products, employees, assets, and equity?

Select Good Agents
1. When selecting agents, do you thoroughly assess quality of service?
2. Do you routinely conduct a cost-benefit analysis of agent services?
3. Do you perform reference checks on agents?
4. Does your agent give you first-line, high-profile service?
5. Does your agent want your business?

Those Compelled
1. Are your products hard to sell?
2. Are you at the mercy of your suppliers?
3. How long does it take to sell your products?
4. Are you in a competitive market?
5. Do you have opportunities to offer new products and services?

Greed Makes a Slave
1. Do you spend too much time counting money?
2. Are you always thinking of ways to better serve your customers?
3. Do you grow because of superior products and a desire to serve more people?
4. Have you refused a sale because of ethical or moral reasons?
5. Are you concerned about image and prestige?

Pursue Good Fortune
1. Do you like what you do?
2. Is what you do valuable or do you add value because of what you do?
3. Do you charge enough and are you fairly compensated for your efforts?
4. Are you always looking for new opportunities?
5. How has your life changed over the years?

Gifts and Rebates
1. Do you remember significant dates, such as birthdays and anniversaries, for your key suppliers and customers?
2. Do you give meaningful gifts to key suppliers and customers?
3. Do you offer rebates to buyers on a regular basis?
4. Do you know the value of the gifts and rebates you offer?
5. Do you tell people thank you?

Spend Less Than You Make
1. Do you reinvest in your company?
2. Do you save a portion of what you earn?
3. Are your expenses necessary?
4. Do you find joy in the little things?
5. Are you building assets for the future?

Keep Within Bounds
1. Does the company's debt exceed its equity?
2. Do you risk the company's health by

participating in all-or-nothing deals and ventures?

3. Are there areas of risk that have not been thoroughly investigated?
4. Are partners capable of "sinking the ship?"
5. Do you feel the urgency to be a mover and shaker?

Bibliography

Abu al-Fadl Ja'far ibn 'Ali al-Dimishqi. "Advice to the Merchants of Medieval Damascus." *The World of Business.* Boston: Harvard Business Publishing; New York: Simon and Schuster, 1962: 184–190.

Adelson, Howard L. *Medieval Commerce.*, Princeton, NJ: D. Van Hostrand, 1962.

Aesop. *Fables of Aesop.* Translated by S.A. Handford. London: Penguin Books, 1964: 23.

Bacon, Francis. *The Essays.* Edited by John Pitcher. London: Penguin Books, 1985: 165, 203–204.

Calhoun, George M. *The Business Life of Ancient Athens.* New York: Cooper Square Publishers, 1968: 95–124.

Franklin, Benjamin. *The Autobiography of Benjamin Franklin & Selections from His Other Writings.* Modern Library ed. New York: Random House, 1950: 232–234.

Gardner, Martin. *The Scientific American Book of Mathematical Puzzles & Diversions.* New York: Simon and Schuster, 1959: 89–90.

Geneen, Harold and Alvin Moscow. *Managing.* New York: Doubleday, 1984: 181–196.

Iacocca, Lee. *Iacocca: An Autobiography.* With William Novak. New York: Bantam, 1984: 64.

Strieder, Jacob. *Jacob Fugger the Rich: Merchant and Banker of Augsburg, 1459–1525.* Edited by N.S.B. Gras. Translated by Mildred L. Hartsough. Hamden, CT: Archon Books, 1966.

Tacitus. *The Annals of Imperial Rome*. Translated by
Michael Grant. London: Penguin Books, 1989: 245–255,
278, 280–284.

Tranquillus, Gaius Suetonius. *The Twelve Caesars*.
Translated by Robert Graves. London: Penguin Books, 1989:
204–205, 207–208, 280.

Tzu, Sun. *The Art of War*. Translated by Samuel B. Griffith.
London: Oxford University, 1963: 144–149.

Walton, Sam. *Sam Walton, Made in America: My Story*.
With John Huey. New York: Doubleday, 1992: 25.

The Holy Bible: King James Version. LDS ed. Salt Lake
City: Church of Jesus Christ of Latter-day Saints. 1984:
Genesis 41:37–41.

FIRE and Other Stuff chronicles author Gaylen K. Bunker's forty-plus years in the finance industry, his experiences in the workplace, the circumstances in which many finance professionals encounter, and the lessons he has learned, which he now teaches to students as a professor of finance at Westminster College in Salt Lake City.

Set in Constantinople, Turkey, *The Merchant* tells the story of Matthew, a young, aspiring entrepreneur and his reluctant mentor, Abu, who through some difficult lessons, instills in Matthew the ten principles of a successful merchant.

Made in the USA
Lexington, KY
18 May 2011